AN INTRODUCTION TO
ARGENTINA

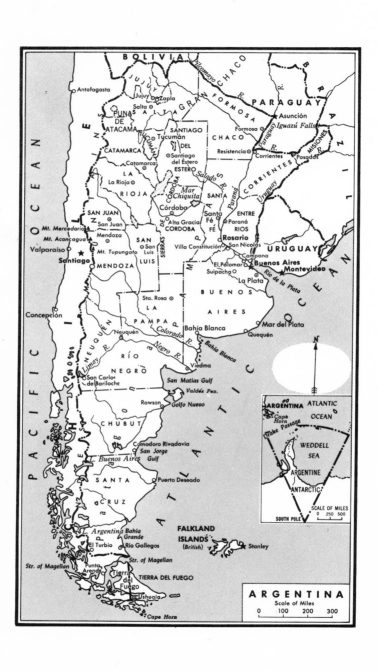

ARGENTINA

Scale of Miles

0   100   200   300

An
Introduction
to
Argentina

Robert J. Alexander

FREDERICK A. PRAEGER, *Publishers*
New York · Washington · London

FREDERICK A. PRAEGER, PUBLISHERS
111 Fourth Avenue, New York, N.Y. 10003, U.S.A.
5, Cromwell Place, London S.W.7, England

Published in the United States of America in 1969
by Frederick A. Praeger, Publishers

To

MONROE BERKOWITZ

Preface

My personal acquaintance with Argentina goes back more than twenty years. At the time of my first visit, in 1946, President Juan Perón was newly in office and was still governing more or less as a democratic ruler. On various occasions, I made other visits to Argentina during the Perón regime, and later under the administrations of Presidents Aramburu, Frondizi, and Illia. The last of these visits was made only a week before the coup that overthrew President Illia and imposed the military dictatorship of President Juan Carlos Onganía.

In the past, too, I have dealt with Argentina in several books. My first published volume was a study of the Perón regime, one of the first such books to be published in the United States. Another volume dealt with the system of labor relations that was largely developed under Perón and that continued largely intact under subsequent regimes. Finally, in my book *Prophets of the Revolution,* I devoted a chapter to Juan Perón.

However, I never before tried to write a volume giving an over-all view of the Argentine Republic. I therefore welcomed the invitation of my long-time friend Víctor Alba to write such a book for publication by Frederick A. Praeger, Inc. The present volume is the result of this invitation..

The writing of this book was a considerable challenge. For several years, I have been puzzled and dismayed by the continuing crisis that has plagued Argentina, which its leaders and people have seemed unable to resolve. Many Argentine intellectuals and political leaders have been equally puzzled. Therefore, it was perhaps somewhat rash of me to attempt to offer in this small volume even a tentative explanation of why this crisis occurred and why it has lasted so long and to suggest how it may finally end. I hope that the readers of the book will not be too critical of my efforts, because I feel that I have correctly outlined at least some of the roots of the answers to these problems.

This book, like all others, did not emerge full-blown from the mind of its author. Many other people contributed to it, and the author owes debts of gratitude to a number of people associated with it in one way or another.

First of all, I owe an unpayable obligation to the innumerable Argentines and students of Argentine affairs with whom I have talked over the last two decades. The great majority of them showed patience and kindness in the face of my continual questioning, the extent of which only they can realize. Many of these people I consider today to be good friends.

Second, I wish to thank Víctor Alba for inviting me to write the work. Similarly, I want to express my appreciation to Louis Barron of Praeger for his help in connection with seeing it through the process of publication. Likewise, I am indebted to Emma Wenz and Mary Carman, who typed the original manuscript.

Finally, like most authors, I owe a large debt to my family —my wife, Joan Alexander, and my children, Tony and Meg —who tolerated me during the writing of this volume. They have put up with my spending much time typing when, in their view, I might well have been doing other, more productive things. I hope that the results will be such as to make them think that my preoccupation with this job has at least some justification.

ROBERT J. ALEXANDER

Rutgers University
New Brunswick, New Jersey

Contents

AN INTRODUCTION TO
ARGENTINA

Introduction—The Problem

The recent history of Argentina has been tragic. It is a tale of lost opportunities, of frustrated aspirations and ambitions, of economic decline, political confusion bordering on anarchy, mounting social problems, and plummeting international prestige. For almost four decades, the country has been going through an economic, political, social, cultural, and, most of all, a moral crisis.

A fundamental aspect of the agonizing Argentine crisis is economic. Economic growth and development have been insufficient to keep the expansion of the national income ahead of the relatively slow population growth. For two decades, the country has been faced with a mounting inflation that has not been offset by the one factor that might justify it, the rapid development of the economy. At the same time, much of the capital equipment that the country possessed in the early 1930's—railroads, roads, and many of the public utilities—has been allowed to deteriorate.

Another basic element of the Argentine crisis, and perhaps the most important one of all, is political. Since 1930, the nation has lived through an unending series of political disturbances, with periods of dictatorship relieved intermittently by limited intervals of constitutional democracy. An endless series of coups and countercoups has frustrated, bewildered, and baffled the average citizen and even most of the politicians.

The crisis in cultural affairs has likewise been grave. The

3

proud leadership in this field, which Argentina once afforded to the rest of Latin America, has been seriously undermined, if not destroyed. The quality of Argentina's educational system, particularly the universities, has been imperiled by purges and counterpurges for more than a quarter of a century. Many of the country's most talented scientists and intellectuals have been driven to seek refuge abroad, and this "brain drain" has become a serious impediment to the economic as well as to the cultural development of the country.

All of these problems have robbed Argentina of the leading position it once had among the Latin American states. Where once it was a model to be followed or at least carefully studied by other Latin American countries striving for political stability, it is now widely regarded as a horrible case of what should not be done, of errors to be avoided. Although some of its neighbors may still have a lingering fear of Argentina's potential imperialist aspirations, few Latin American nations look to it for leadership.

Argentina's record since 1930 is the more disturbing because of the substantial resources with which the country is endowed and the initial advantages it possessed. Argentina has some of the world's richest agricultural land in its great flat plains, the pampas. It has sufficient petroleum reserves to serve its own needs for many decades to come and to make it a substantial exporter. Although Argentina's presently known mineral resources are modest, there is reason to believe that its potentialities in this respect are great. The country has in Buenos Aires one of the world's most strategically located ports.

That is not all. For the most part, Argentina's climate is a healthy one and its people do not suffer from the difficulties of overcoming the disadvantages of excessive tropical heat. Its population is relatively homogeneous, and there are not the deep racial conflicts that plague those Latin American countries with a large Indian population. To a less degree than in most other Latin American nations is its population polarized between a very wealthy upper class and the poverty-stricken masses; it has the largest middle class in the hemisphere outside of the United States and Canada, and many of those who are not formally regarded as members of the middle class have a middle-class outlook and value system. For three generations, Argentina has had the most literate populace of any nation in Latin America.

Furthermore, for a period of nearly fifty years, until 1930, Argentina seemed to be a model of economic prosperity and political stability. During this epoch, it developed a cattle- and grain-exporting economy that made possible one of the highest standards of living anywhere in the world. At the same time, Argentina went for fifty years without any successful attempts to overthrow the government by unconstitutional means (and with fairly few *un*successful ones).

Since 1930, the Argentine record has been an unhappy one. The amount of land used for agriculture and grazing has declined drastically. Industrialization has progressed only by fits and starts. Argentina's long experience of political stability has been replaced by something approaching record instability. Its cultural life has stagnated and even deteriorated, despite progress in some fields.

What is the explanation for this startling contrast between promise and achievement? Fundamentally, the fault lies in the inability of Argentine leaders and people to carry out with any degree of consistency the changes in institutions and in private and public policies that are necessary if Argentina is to make the transition from a rural-based society and economy controlled by aristocratic landowners to a modern diversified economy and a highly mobile society.

There are many facets to this problem. One of them is that the rural aristocracy has continued to wield a degree of power and influence in public life far out of proportion to its numerical importance in the population and even to its significance in the country's economic life. Another important element is that Argentine public opinion has never wholly accepted the need for rapid economic development, particularly industrialization. Even in the 1960's, there is a respectable current of opinion that sees the country's salvation much more in terms of a revival of the halcyon days of wheat and meat prosperity before 1930 than in the development of a diversified and balanced economy.

Most fundamental of all is the fact that no middle-class political leadership has evolved that could mobilize effectively both the middle and lower classes around a program of reform and rapid economic development. A group that sought to exercise such leadership would have to have a program that not only sought the transformation of the country's economic structure through the stimulation of industrialization, but also supported the legitimate demands of lower-class groups—the rural and urban workers—for redress of their long-suffered grievances.

The first middle-class government of Argentina came to power in 1916, when the broadly based Radical Party elected its leader, Hipólito Irigoyen, to the presidency. However, during the fourteen years in which the Radical Party held the reins of government, it did little, if anything, to stimulate industrialization and diversification of the economy, to enact social and labor legislation, or to carry out the even more fundamental job of giving the workers, particularly the urban workers, the feeling that they really had some say and participation in the government. Furthermore, the Radical administrations suffered to an exceptional degree from the vices of patronage and corruption, which tended to discredit them in the eyes of even their own middle-class followers.

Thus, the lower classes became disillusioned with the Radicals as a result of their first experience with a middle-class government in power, and they voiced little protest when it was overthrown, in September, 1930, by a military coup that marked the beginning of a thirteen-year period in which power was once again exercised principally by the old rural aristocracy.

It was Colonel Juan Domingo Perón who next tried to bring about an effective middle-class and lower-class alliance. He only partially succeeded. Although he won the allegiance and support of a strong majority of the urban and rural working class, his success among the middle class was limited. Some middle-class elements were alienated by Perón's obvious attempts to use the workers as a base for advancing his own interests; others turned against him because of the increasingly dictatorial proclivities of his regime.

Perón's seizure of leadership in the movement for social reform and economic development introduced another element that complicated the needed transformation of Argentina's economy and society. The Perón regime tended to create an all but unbridgeable gulf between Peronistas and anti-Peronistas in the Argentine body politic. This resulted in the formation of new alliances against him among people who had started out from entirely different points on the country's political spectrum and who held vastly different opinions on the fundamental questions of social reform and industrialization. The landed aristocracy, fearful of the impact of Perón's social and economic program, were joined by very large segments of the middle class that resented his political dictatorship; both of these made common cause with military men who, for a wide variety of reasons, both private and public, were opposed to Perón.

More than a decade of common struggle against the Perón regime resulted in many of these disparate elements remaining united even after Perón was overthrown, in September, 1955. Moreover, memories of the dictatorship, as well as Perón's fiery promises that heads would roll by the thousands when and if he returned to the presidency, created in the hearts and minds of most anti-Peronistas the uncompromising and unalterable determination that he would under no circumstances be allowed to return to power.

All of the post-Perón history of Argentina, then, can be understood only in terms of two basic issues: that of continuing the change in the nation's social and economic institutions begun by Perón; and that of his possible return to power. To obtain the former, any regime needed the co-operation of the Peronistas; yet this could not be gained so long as a party or an administration took the position that the latter was under no circumstances permissible. Each successive regime since 1955 has foundered on its inability to resolve these two mutually exclusive problems.

The most serious effort since 1955 to grapple with these issues was made by the administration of Arturo Frondizi (1958–62). Raising once again the banner of rapid economic development and eventual social reform, and having at first the tacit support of the Peronistas, Frondizi ultimately foundered when he returned to the Peronistas the more or less full exercise of their political rights, and thus ran the risk that in the foreseeable future they might be able to win control of the country and bring back Perón. The government of President Arturo Illia (1963–66), which showed little enthusiasm for the economic-development programs launched by Frondizi, fell on the same issue of incorporating the Peronistas into the country's political life.

Thus, it is against the background of the struggle over structural changes in the economy and society, and over the possible return of Perón, that the prolonged Argentine crisis should be envisioned. The reader who peruses the chapters that follow, which picture both the rich potentialities of the country and the failure of its people to make the best of these potentialities, should keep these two basic problems constantly in mind. In the concluding chapter, I shall try to give some indication of how Argentina's forty-year-old crisis may perhaps be resolved.

I

The Land

It is an unforgettable experience to fly over the great pampas of central Argentina. One can fly westward for hours over the flatness beneath, stretching to the outer limits of the horizon, changing only in its color, shading slowly from deep green into yellowish brown. Then, suddenly, as one looks ahead, the glacier-capped majesty of the Andean mountain range suddenly comes into view, extending to the right and left as far as one can see.

Such a trip reveals only one facet of the diversity of Argentina's geography. On the map, the country appears like an inverted triangle. Its wide base extends across the semitropical middle of South America near the Tropic of Capricorn, and the rest of the triangle narrows down almost to a point in the island of Tierra del Fuego, only a few hundred miles from Antarctica. Argentina occupies almost one-third of the South American continent and is 2,150 miles long and 980 miles across at its widest point. Its total area is 1,072,745 square miles, which makes it about one-third the size of the United States. Argentina is bordered by the Andes, which separate it from Chile on the west; by Bolivia on the northwest, from which it is not divided by any natural barriers; by Paraguay, Brazil, and Uruguay, which lie across the Paraguay and Paraná rivers on the northeast; by the Atlantic Ocean on the east; and by the Antarctic Ocean on the south. It consists of most of the old Spanish viceroyalty of the Río de la Plata, from which only the one-time provinces of Upper Peru (Bolivia) and Paraguay withdrew during the wars of independence.

The pampas are the part of Argentina best known abroad. They stretch with monotonous flatness from the Atlantic Ocean and the Río de la Plata estuary westward for as much as 400 miles to the foothills of the Andes. Much of the region is neatly demarcated by barbed-wire fences separating one great *estancia* from another. The pampas are the home of the gaucho, the Argentine cowboy of fact and fiction, and today the great majority of the nation's people live there, amid the rich grain fields and the lush grazing pastures. Most of the country's major cities are located in the pampas, and across them run most of Argentina's railroads and highways.

The pampas are the largest and richest of Argentina's four major geographical regions. In addition to this great central-plains region, there is the great span of the Andes, the wide and diversified north, and the largely arid and cold southern quarter of the country, known as Patagonia. These regions are differentiated by variations in altitude, climatic conditions, and vegetation. In the extreme west, the great Andes mountain chain is the defining feature, sloping down to wide plateaus in the northwest; in the center of the country, the great alluvial plains; in the south, the dry, cold plateau. Other features include the river system, comprising the famous Río de la Plata estuary and its tributaries—the Paraná, Paraguay, and Uruguay rivers, which together provide one of the major means of penetration into the heart of the continent. These rivers are also a means of communication between Buenos Aires and a large part of the interior, and form part of Argentina's boundary with Uruguay, Paraguay, and Brazil.

The geographical divisions of the country also depend in large part on the people who live in them, as Preston James, perhaps the leading authority on Latin American geography,

has stressed. For example, "the divisions of a frontier territory commonly recognized by the settlers themselves are the
areas served by the different routes of access. The people
living in the Argentine humid pampa still think of themselves in the zone of this or that railroad line."*

The Andes

The Andes, the world's second highest mountain range,
extend like a backbone down the length of western Argentina. In the northwestern part of the country, Preston James
notes, there is little to distinguish the region from neighboring parts of Bolivia. Altitudes generally rise to between
11,000 and 13,000 feet in the intermediate area between the
high plateaus of the Andes and the low-lying Chaco region.
Here the country is cut by deep river valleys as well as by
some broader valleys known as *quebradas,* historically the
routes of penetration from the Atlantic coast to the high
Andes. Interspersed in this area are isolated higher mountains, with peaks reaching as high as 19,000 feet. Bordering
on the Chaco and reaching south to the area around Tucumán is a region of somewhat lower altitudes, interspersed
by valleys running north and south.

It is in this northwestern region that most of Argentina's
mining takes place. Although mining does not loom large
in the total economy of Argentina—and a curious geological
fact is the paucity of mineral resources found on the eastern
side of the Andes in contrast to the extensive mineral wealth
that has been discovered and exploited in Chile—there are
many little mining centers in northwestern Argentina. The
country is an important producer of asbestos and beryllium,
and there are also deposits of lead, zinc, copper, silver, tung-
sten, and other minerals. A bit farther south, in the Province
of Salta, is located the country's second largest group of oil
fields.

* Preston James, *Latin America* (New York: The Odyssey Press, 1959), p. 299.

The imposing Andean mountain range narrows markedly as one approaches central Argentina. In some areas, the boundary with Chile runs along the crest of the range, while elsewhere it veers over to the east, with only the piedmont area remaining within Argentina. The region contains some of the world's highest peaks, including the highest in the Western Hemisphere—Mount Aconcagua, at 23,034 feet. During the winter months, vast white storms whirl through the valleys; during the summer, some of the mountains, bare of snow, loom like mammoth pieces of jagged rock, with their sharp edges reaching toward the sky, though many are snow-covered all year around.

East of the mountains, the sub-Andean foothills slant slowly down to the pampas and Patagonia. The piedmont area west of the pampas is very arid, with only a few irrigated and oasis areas, such as those around Mendoza, Catamarca, and San Juan.

The North

The Argentine north divides logically into two subregions, the Chaco and the so-called Mesopotamia area. The first of these lies just east of the Andes, while Mesopotamia gets its name from the fact that it is located between the Paraná and Uruguay rivers, which naturally suggested to early settlers the parallel with the Middle Eastern region lying between the Tigris and Euphrates.

The Argentine Chaco is part of a much wider area, which includes northern Paraguay, parts of western Brazil, and eastern Bolivia. The region is a great alluvial plain, its soil composed of deposits washed down from the Andes by numerous rivers. During the rainy season, the streams that cut through the Chaco overflow their banks and flood wide areas, especially those near the Pilcomayo, Bermejo, Salado, and Dule rivers. They frequently change course, sometimes shifting after each yearly flood. Near the Paraná River, in the eastern part, the floodwaters are often no more than a foot deep, so that railroad embankments and clusters of houses stand up above the flood level.

The Chaco is a woodland region—consisting for the most part of deciduous scrub trees, which sometimes grow so densely as to make it very difficult for people to pass through them—dotted with small areas of grassy savannah. Temperatures in the Chaco tend to be high, particularly in the summertime, comparable to those along the Gulf Coast of the United States. These high temperatures mean rapid evaporation, and, in spite of 20–50 inches of rainfall a year, settled agriculture is virtually impossible without irrigation.

The principal sources of wealth in the Chaco region are the quebracho forests in its western part and cotton in its eastern part. The quebracho, a small tree of the sumac family, is the source of tannin, valuable for processing leather. It has been exploited for more than 100 years and was the first thing to attract settlers to this barren region. Cotton-growing is relatively new to the Chaco, having developed only in the 1930's. In that period, many immigrants— among them Spaniards and Slavs—settled in the region, mostly in areas the quebracho cutters had cleared. This movement of population was sufficiently large to justify the transformation of the Chaco from a federal territory into a province in the late 1940's.

Mesopotamia includes the western end of the Paraná plateau as well as a large lowland area. The territory of Misiones, a long tongue of Argentine land that juts up eastward between Paraguay and Brazil, shares with those two countries one of the great natural wonders of the Western Hemisphere, the magnificent Iguazú Falls. Misiones is also the Argentine center of production of the bitter tea made from the yerba maté plant, a favorite drink in the Río de la Plata area.

Farther west, in the provinces of Entre Ríos and Corrientes, there are extensive grazing lands, which not only support cattle but have made the region a rival of Patagonia in the raising of sheep. And there are some regions near the pampas where corn and flax are important products.

Patagonia

Patagonia is a vast arid plain lying below the Río Colorado, cut at infrequent intervals by deep canyons, some of which have streams that run during all or part of the year but many of which are dry. For the most part, Patagonia is a bleak area, relatively dry, with fierce winds blowing over it most of the time. Only in a few of the canyon-valleys is there sufficient protection from the wind to maintain agriculture. These valleys are green with vegetation and present a sharp contrast to the grayness of most of the region. Elsewhere, sheep-herding is the major occupation.

In spite of the fact that cloudy weather is frequent in much of Patagonia and fogs often hover over much of its southern part, rainfall is exceedingly sparse, in some parts as low as 4–5 inches a year. This fact, together with the low temperature, makes the area generally inhospitable to man. As a result, although it comprises one-quarter of the area of Argentina, Patagonia has only about 1 per cent of its population.

Patagonia was not opened for permanent settlement until the end of the Indian wars in the 1880's. Since there were few natural harbors and few resources to encourage trade and settlement, sheep-herding developed as the most logical economic activity. As a result, people with experience in this kind of work moved to Patagonia, including not only Argentines from the pampas and other regions but also foreign immigrants—from the Chilean area of Punta Arenas on the Straits of Magellan and from England, Scotland, and Wales. (Many of the descendants of the British immigrants still speak English.)

Sheep-herding does not require very many workers. One lonely shepherd can tend a large number of animals. Even the work involved in shearing wool and preparing it for shipment does not require many hands. In Patagonia sheep-herding is organized on huge estates, some of which encompass thousands of square miles. The workers and their families live in small villages near the headquarters of the estate, and here the dipping and shearing is done. The wool is then dispatched to any one of several small ports, whence it is shipped to Buenos Aires and other centers of the textile industry.

In recent decades, some new lines of economic activity have been developed in Patagonia. Soon after the turn of the century, oil was discovered near Comodoro Rivadavia, on the San Jorge Gulf, and by the 1920's this had become Argentina's chief center of petroleum production. Subsequently, oil was also discovered at Plaza Huincal in the Province of Neuquén. During the Perón period, when extensive explorations for new minerals were conducted throughout the country, large quantities of low-grade coal were discovered at Río Turbio, in the foothills of the Andes, and those areas have since been opened up for exploitation despite the high costs involved in transporting the coal to the markets in the central part of the country.

The Pampas

The pampas are the heartland of Argentina. They are the demographic, economic, political, and cultural center of the nation. The other three areas which we have described are little more than a periphery to the great plains that have provided Argentina with most of its wealth and where most of the inhabitants live.

The pampas cover what is said to be one of the oldest land areas on the globe. Their bedrock of granite and other crystalline rocks is throughout most of the region buried far beneath a rich alluvial cover. Near Buenos Aires, the cover is 985 feet deep. (There are only a few places where the bedrock comes near the surface: on the Sierra del Tandil, which rises 1,600 feet above the surrounding area, and on the Sierra de la Ventana, which is 4,200 feet higher than the plains around.) The strong winds that blow from time to time across the pampas are not as violent as those of Patagonia, but over thousands of years they have been to a considerable degree responsible for depositing an additional layer of very rich and porous soil that is characteristic of these plains. Because of the alluvial and aeolian nature of the soil, there are virtually no rocks, pebbles, or gravel to be found.

Inhabitants of the pampas distinguish between the various winds—the *norte,* which is hot and sultry, and the *pampero,* the cooler and more comfortable wind that comes from the south across the plains. Because of these winds, the weather of Buenos Aires and of most of the pampas is variable. When the cool air from the south meets warmer and more humid air from the tropical regions, they produce clouds and rain. At the point of contact, there are frequent thunderstorms: "The territory around Buenos Aires is noted for the violence of its thunderstorms and the magnificence of its displays of lightning."*

The pampas have mild winters and hot summers. The summer temperature of Buenos Aires is comparable to that of New York, although the winters of the Argentine capital are milder. The average July temperature in Buenos Aires is 48.9° F., and the average January temperature is 73.6° F.

The pampas are the principal area in which cattle and grain are produced. Wheat is grown in a great crescent extending from Sante Fé along the western edge of the pampas to an area just east of Bahía Blanca, in the southern part of the Province of Buenos Aires. The amount of wheat grown varies sharply from one year to the other, depending upon

* Preston James , *Latin America,* p. 328.

the price of the grain. Other grains grown in the pampas are maize, barley, and flax, of which maize is certainly the most important. The growing of maize is largely concentrated in an area centering on the port of Rosario, on the Paraná River. The amount of land devoted to it reached its largest extension in the mid-1930's and thereafter declined. Although the Frondizi administration sought to stimulate maize cultivation, production has not yet returned to what it was in its heyday. Indeed, the extent of land in Argentina devoted to grain cultivation in general has been declining since the high point of the 1930's. In the late 1960's, it was only a little more than half of what it had been twenty-five years before.

Cattle are grazed widely throughout the pampas. In no part of the region is the percentage of land devoted to grazing less than 40 per cent, and in much of the pampas it rises to 80 per cent. (There is some tendency for the use of the land to alternate between grazing and grain production, depending on the relative prices of the two kinds of products.) Dairying is an increasingly important aspect of the cattle industry, particularly in the region southeast of Buenos Aires. Near Buenos Aires, both cattle and grain production have been giving way to truck gardening for the capital's growing market.

Traditionally, the pampas have been an area of large landholdings. In the late 1950's, there were still fifty families in the Province of Buenos Aires, each of whose estates consisted of more than 75,000 acres. However, several forces have been working in the direction of breaking up some of these estates. One of these has been the inheritance laws, which provide that all children shall benefit equally as heirs, although many landowning families have sought to combat this by forming corporations to hold their properties. Another factor has been the incapacity for business of some of the owners. Finally, a number of private land companies, faced with low prices and rising labor costs, have been selling off part of their holdings to small farmers. But these tendencies have not yet gone far enough to change the fundamental picture. The continuation of the large landownership pattern has meant that the social and political importance of the rural aristocracy has continued to be considerable, a major factor in the country's nearly four decades of political instability and intermittent military dictatorship.

Urban Areas

Argentina was the first country of Latin America to become predominantly urban in population, and by the late 1940's, 57 per cent of the total populace lived in cities and towns of more than 5,000 people. Most of Argentina's estimated 23 million people, and most of its largest cities, are located in, or on the edges of, the pampas. Overshadowing all Argentine cities is Buenos Aires, the nation's capital and principal manufacturing and commercial center. The federal capital, or the city of Buenos Aires proper, had, in 1965, a population estimated at some 3,226,900. In addition, the capital is the center of a hub of smaller, but still considerable municipalities. Greater Buenos Aires has a total population of over 5 million, or approximately 25 per cent of the Argentine total.

Buenos Aires is also the nation's principal transportation hub. It is the main port for the Río de la Plata river complex, serving much of the interior of South America. The rivers draining into the Río de la Plata estuary serve most of northern Argentina, as well as all of Paraguay, and parts of Uruguay, Brazil, and Bolivia. Since most of Argentina's railroads were constructed to bring the grains and meat of the pampas to the ports from which they were shipped to Europe, they have tended to radiate from Rosario and Buenos Aires, particularly the latter. Most of the rail lines fan out from the port-capital over the pampas—westward toward Mendoza and other cities in the foothills of the Andes; north toward Rosario and Córdoba and ultimately toward the frontier areas bordering on Paraguay, Brazil, and Bolivia; and south toward Bahía Blanca.

In the Buenos Aires area are concentrated many of the nation's manufacturing enterprises—particularly its metallurgical and textile industries. Cement, chemicals, meat-packing, grain-milling, and leather-working are among the other important kinds of manufacturing in greater Buenos Aires. Commerce and finance are other activities centered in Buenos Aires. Situated on the Plata estuary, the city is Argentina's largest port and the seat of many large firms handling not only the import and export trade but also the internal distribution of products.

Finally, the great bulk of the governmental bureaucracy works in Buenos Aires and lives there or in the neighboring towns and cities. Also, the heaviest concentrations of armed forces are located in and around Buenos Aires.

Some fifty miles southeast of Buenos Aires is the city of La Plata, specially built to be capital of the Province of Buenos Aires, when the port city was separated from the province in the 1880's. It is an important center of the meat-packing industry. Farther south in the Province of Buenos Aires lie Mar del Plata, the country's principal seaside vacation spa, and Bahía Blanca, an important port and naval base. Argentina possesses very few cities along its long Atlantic coastline because there are very few good natural ports. Even Buenos Aires has an artificial harbor that must be dredged regularly. Bahía Blanca and the oil port of Comodoro Rivadavia, in Patagonia, are among the few exceptions. In the northeastern part of the province is the city of San Nicolás, which has gained new importance since the establishment there of the country's first major steel plant in the early 1950's.

Various cities in the interior are also of significance.

Rosario, on the Paraná River, 200 miles from Buenos Aires, has a population estimated, in 1965, at about 675,000 and is the nation's second largest port. It is a major center of grain-milling, meat-packing, and various other manufacturing industries. Northwest of Rosario is Córdoba, with some 600,000 people, an old university town and cultural center, which, in recent years, has become an important industrial town with the establishment there of automobile, agricultural-implement, and airplane-manufacturing plants. Tucumán, directly north of Córdoba, in the Andean foothills, is the chief center of the sugar-refining industry, while Mendoza, almost 400 miles west of Buenos Aires, is the nation's principal wine-producing center.

II

Historical Background

The first Europeans to set foot on the land of present-day Argentina were members of a Spanish expedition in 1516, headed by Juan Díaz de Solís, eager to explore and claim the southern part of the continent for the Spanish Crown. Díaz de Solís and many of his followers were attacked by Indians and killed. Eleven years later, in 1527, another Spanish expedition, headed by the Italian navigator Sebastian Cabot, landed near—and named—the Río de la Plata (River of Silver), apparently in the belief that the estuary was a gateway to vast treasures in the interior.

However, most Spaniards who settled within the borders of the present Argentine Republic came down from the west and north—over the mountains from settlements in Peru and Upper Peru (Bolivia). These settlers established Córdoba, Tucumán, and other cities, while other Spaniards came over the Andes from settlements in Chile.

Buenos Aires was not firmly established until 1580. (An earlier attempt by Pedro de Mendoza to found a settlement on the spot in 1536 was abandoned five years later because of Indian attacks.) In 1617, Buenos Aires was made the capital of a province, and finally, in 1776, with the establishment of the new Viceroyalty of La Plata, Buenos Aires was made its capital, thus becoming one of the four major administrative centers of the Spanish Empire in America.

Originally, Spain had attempted to rule her American

21

possessions through the Viceroyalty of Santo Domingo, centered in the West Indies. With the discovery and conquest of huge regions on the American continent, however, the Caribbean headquarters was abandoned and its place taken by the Viceroyalty of New Spain, with headquarters in Mexico City, and the Viceroyalty of Peru, centered in Lima, Peru. Finally, the latter was split into two new viceroyalties —New Granada, with Bogotá as its capital, and La Plata.

Each of these major subdivisions of Spanish America was officially a kingdom, on a hierarchical par with that of Spain itself. They were governed directly by the King of Spain, through the Council of the Indies, with its headquarters in Seville (the only port through which the American possessions of Spain were legally entitled to trade with Europe).

The Viceroyalty of La Plata included considerably more than present-day Argentina, having within its borders the present republics of Bolivia and Paraguay. Contemporary Uruguay was then a border area between Spanish and Portuguese America and changed hands several times during the colonial era, but when under Spanish control it was part of La Plata. The Spaniards also claimed segments of southern Brazil as part of this unit of their empire. During the wars of independence, Bolivia and Paraguay broke away from the old viceroyalty, while Uruguay was fought over by Argentina and Brazil and was finally recognized, in 1828, as an independent buffer state.

Logically, Buenos Aires should have developed into one of the most important ports of the Spanish Empire. It is situated at the mouth of a river system that should have provided a simpler way of getting to Bolivia, parts of Peru, and other interior sectors of the empire than did the long route to Panama and down the Pacific coast. But during most of the colonial period, Buenos Aires suffered at the expense of the economic and political power of the gold- and silver-mining interests in Peru and of the merchants of Lima.

In accordance with the strict mercantilist policies of the Spanish Crown, virtually all trade between Europe and Spanish America was conducted via the convoyed fleets periodically dispatched from Seville or Cádiz to Mexico and Panama. From Panama, goods for South America were transshipped to Lima, whence they were dispersed to other Spanish holdings on the continent. Thus, the cities and towns of Argentina were for more than two centuries supplied with European goods largely through caravans coming over the mountains from Lima. And during much of this period, trade through Buenos Aires or other Atlantic ports was actually forbidden.

Of course, the prohibitions were by no means sufficient to prevent completely trade through the La Plata estuary. Smuggling—largely by the English, Dutch, and French, who were eager to undermine the Spanish system—was rife, and, as a result, Buenos Aires very early had a much larger resident foreign population than did most Spanish-American towns. Still, there is no question that, until the relaxation of Spanish controls in the middle of the eighteenth century, Buenos Aires suffered greatly from the mercantilist policies favoring Lima.

The interior towns and cities of Argentina tended naturally to be oriented toward Peru rather than toward Buenos Aires. In the surrounding areas, some agricultural products and cattle were raised, as well as work animals for use in the Andes mining regions. Mules, the ubiquitous and hardworking animals that could be used not only around the mines but also to carry heavy loads back and forth across the mountains, were of particular importance. Since the mares from which the sterile mules—crosses between horses and jackasses—were bred, survived only with difficulty in the rarefied atmosphere of the high Andes, mules from the lower altitudes of northern Argentina were widely used in Peru and Bolivia.

This trade in animals and agricultural products was not sufficient, however, to supply the inhabitants of the Argentine towns in the interior with all the manufactured goods they needed. As a result, sizable groups of craftsmen grew up in these towns, producing goods for the local market. These artisan groups persisted well into the nineteenth century.

There were a few cities in the La Plata Viceroyalty. The earliest were those of the interior, such as Córdoba, Tucumán, and Santiago del Estero, first established as outposts of the Spanish settlements in the high Andes. As the colonial era drew to a close, Buenos Aires grew more important, having become the principal entrepôt between Europe and the interior of southern South America.

During most of the colonial period, the pampas were largely occupied by Indian tribes engaging in hunting and in shifting agriculture. The pampas also had large herds of wild cattle, which were descendants of animals, brought by early Spanish settlers, that had been abandoned when the first settlements were deserted. In those parts of the plain where the Indians were no longer sovereign, the population consisted principally of gauchos—half-breed cattlemen, culturally not much different from the aborigines and, like the Indians, usually hunters of the wild cattle, some of which they sold to the people of Buenos Aires and other cities.

Another area of settlement was that bordering what is now northern Uruguay, southern Brazil, and Paraguay. There, the Jesuits established missions where they founded schools and brought considerable numbers of Indians together in villages. The Argentine Province of Misiones, to this day, bears a name reflecting this aspect of Argentine history. Jesuit settlements disappeared soon after the banning of the Jesuits from the Spanish Empire in 1767.

Although the Spanish did not hold their Argentine possessions in very high regard, they aroused the avarice of other powers. Thus, in 1806, the British made a strong attack on Buenos Aires, seeking, perhaps, a route of entry into the interior of the continent. The people of Buenos Aires, in public assembly (the *cabildo abierto*), deposed the viceroy and put in charge a French officer, Jacques de Liniers, to lead the struggle against the invaders. After several months' siege, the British force was driven off.

The Early Independence Period

Four years later, on May 25, 1810, with the conquest of Spain by the forces of Napoleon Bonaparte, who named his brother Joseph to be the new king, the residents of Buenos Aires once again met in a *cabildo abierto*. This meeting proclaimed its loyalty to the deposed Bourbon, named a junta to lead the colony, and deposed the viceroy. This struggle, launched in the name of royal legitimacy, was soon transformed into a war for independence.

By 1816, most of Argentina had been cleared of Spanish troops, and, on July 9 of that year, national independence was officially proclaimed by a congress in Tucumán, of which Martín Pueyrredon was the president. In the following year, José de San Martín, a native Argentine but a former officer in the Spanish Army, was named commander of the Argentine forces. Soon thereafter, feeling that the struggle for independence of all Spanish America was indivisible, he led a group of Argentine soldiers across the Andes to join forces with Chilean independence fighters. Together, they defeated Spanish forces at the battles of Chacabuco and Maipú, achieving Chile's independence. San Martín then led his forces north, where they secured the independence of Peru and Bolivia. After a meeting with the Venezuelan Liberator, Simón Bolívar, in Guayaquil, Ecuador, San Martín, disillusioned by the growing dissension among both military and political leaders of the Spanish-American independence movement, resigned his command, returned to Argentina, and soon afterward embarked for Europe, where he lived until his death in 1852.

The first decades of Argentine independence were marked by great instability and a struggle for power between Federalist and Unitarian forces. The former favored the establishment of a federal republic; the latter, a highly centralized government led by Buenos Aires. While the two sides were thus defined in political terms, their struggle was to a large degree an economic one. During the first decades of independence, the economic difference between the interior and the port of Buenos Aires intensified, with the cities and towns of the former anxious to protect their local industries against imported goods from Europe, with which the *porteños* of Buenos Aires were eager to flood them. The struggle also concerned the control over the collection and spending of customs, the new regime's principal source of revenue. The people of Buenos Aires wanted collection of customs to be centered in their city, while the towns of the interior wished to participate in collecting the revenues.

It was not until the cattle- and grain-growing potentialities of the pampas were realized in the last decades of the nineteenth century that Buenos Aires definitely won this economic struggle. Thereafter, many of the interior towns declined; their handicraft industries were decimated; and their importance as trading centers was all but destroyed. Only those cities that turned out goods in great demand in Buenos Aires and the pampas—such as sugar-producing Tucumán and the wine center Mendoza—were able to participate in Argentina's over-all national prosperity in those decades.

However, the Federalist-Unitarian struggle also concerned more subtle matters. Buenos Aires looked outward toward Europe and had a tendency to want to Europeanize the rest of the country. The interior was both conservative and more American (in the hemispheric sense of the word) and sought to protect its values from encroachment by the port city.

The Rosas Dictatorship and After

In 1825, Argentina had adopted a federal constitution, but in the following year the Unitarian leader Bernardo Rivadavia was elected president, and under him a new, highly centralized constitution took effect. Soon afterward, Rivadavia resigned in the face of widespread opposition, and, in 1827, a Federalist, Manuel Dorrego, became president, although in fact his writ did not run beyond the Province of Buenos Aires. Upon the assassination of Dorrego, in 1828, Juan Manuel de Rosas became leader of the Federalists and from then until 1852, Rosas was dictator of Argentina.

Rosas' principal support came from the gauchos. A large landholder himself, he was an expert horseman and could do most of the jobs on an *estancia* as well as his followers. But, like a typical *estancia*-owner he allowed no one to challenge his rule. Some of his supporters attempted physically to exterminate the Unitarian opponents of his regime. And, although a reasonably well-educated man, Rosas was particularly ruthless against the intellectuals, who were his most persistent opponents. He had a thoroughgoing secret police force, and his enemies were beaten up and killed. Exile was virtually the only way to escape his vengeance.

While Rosas controlled Argentine affairs—during most of which time he was officially only governor of the Province of Buenos Aires—he twice had to fight off foreign invasions. In 1838, a French fleet blockaded Buenos Aires but was driven off. In 1848–49, a joint Anglo-French fleet blockaded the Argentine capital and landed troops in an effort to open up transport on the Paraná and Paraguay rivers, which Rosas had closed to foreign traffic. After a long siege, the foreigners were again driven away.

Rosas also became embroiled in quarrels with his neighbors. Particularly, he sought to gain control of Uruguay and its capital, Montevideo, whose independence had been recognized by Argentina and Brazil in 1828. But he was unable to expand the territory under his control.

The Rosas dictatorship was finally overthrown in 1852, after an insurrection led by one of Rosas' former lieutenants, Justo José de Urquiza. A constitutional convention met in Santa Fé, in 1853, and wrote the constitution that has been in effect ever since (except for a short period between 1949 and 1955, when Perón's administration had one of its own).

However, the Province of Buenos Aires refused to accept General Urquiza's government, which set up its capital in Paraná, and as a result existed as a separate country for several years. In 1859, war broke out between the Argentine Confederation and Buenos Aires, and although, at first, Buenos Aires was defeated, in 1861, when the struggle was renewed, the troops of Buenos Aires, led by General Bartolomé Mitre, won a decisive victory. The country was reunited, and the capital was returned to Buenos Aires.

For almost twenty years, the nation continued in peace under a remarkable series of presidents: Bartolomé Mitre, Domingo Faustino Sarmiento, and Nicolás Avellaneda. All three men had been strong opponents of Rosas. Mitre was a distinguished soldier but also one of Argentina's most distinguished historians and the founder of the newspaper *La Nación*. Sarmiento was a schoolteacher and author, his most famous saying being, "To rule is to educate." Avellaneda was a lawyer and one of the great advocates of large-scale immigration into Argentina. During their administrations, two important developments occurred. The first was the virtual completion of the conquest of the Indians who had controlled most of the southern pampas and Patagonia. The land taken from the Indians was divided among the officers and soldiers of the conquering armies, and these grants, together with those which Rosas had made earlier to various of his followers, contributed to the establishment of the large landholding system that has characterized the pampas ever since.

The second major development was the establishment of the nation's system of public education. President Sarmiento took the lead in this. During his years in exile under Rosas, Sarmiento had visited the United States and had come to know the great American educator Horace Mann. Upon becoming president of Argentina, he turned to Mann and, with his help, recruited a force of Yankee schoolmarms who laid the foundation of what was to become the best public-school system in Latin America.

This period was also marked by one of the few wars that Argentina has ever fought. It was the so-called War of the Triple Alliance, in which Argentina, Uruguay, and Brazil were aligned against Paraguay in a conflict provoked by the ambitions of the Paraguayan dictator Francisco Solano López for hegemony over southern South America. The Paraguayans invaded parts of northern Argentina but were driven out, and most of the rest of the war took place on Paraguayan soil. Although defeated by the alliance—to which Brazil made the major contribution in men and money—the Paraguayans fought to the bitter end, and by the time the conflict was over, virtually all adult Paraguayan males had been killed.

In 1880, the struggle between Buenos Aires and the interior provinces erupted again when President Avellaneda sought to impose as his successor General Julio Roca, who had the support of the interior. When the *porteños* resisted Roca's candidacy and began to train volunteers to resist him, Avellaneda fled the city, and the conflict began. General Roca led the provincial forces, soon made short shrift of the opposition in Buenos Aires, and became president. One of his first acts was to decree the separation of the city of Buenos Aires from its province and its conversion into federal territory. Shortly afterward, the town of La Plata was named capital of the Province of Buenos Aires.

Another major political decision made during the Roca

administration concerned relations between Church and state. By a law of 1884, it was determined that public education should be secular, that no religious instruction should be given in public schools, and that university education should be completely in the hands of the state.

The Birth of the Meat and Grain Economy

With the re-establishment of peace under Roca began the rapid expansion of the Argentine economy which, within one generation, made Argentina the most prosperous nation in Latin America. The pampas were the heart of the economy. Much of their topsoil was of extraordinary depth and richness and lent itself to growing wheat, corn, and other grains, year after year, with little need for fertilization or soil protection. Other parts of the pampas were ideal for growing rich grasses that provided fine feed for cattle.

Although the pampas had always been a potential producer of meat and wheat, the rapid development of modern grazing and grain-growing techniques from 1860 to 1914 was largely influenced by events in Europe and Argentina. In 1846, Great Britain had repealed its Corn Laws which had been designed to prevent the entry of foreign grain into the country.* This meant that Great Britain had decided to concentrate on the production of industrial goods, which it produced more cheaply and in greater quantity than any other nation during that period. It also meant that Great Britain would depend upon other countries, such as Argentina, for foodstuffs and raw materials.

Simultaneously, several developments took place in Ar-

* The repeal of the Corn Laws stepped up the rate of British industrialization and the flow of people to the cities. At the same time, the population of Great Britain was increasing rapidly, and Great Britain had to buy large quantities of foodstuffs from overseas. The United States was the first country to become a supplier to Great Britain. Later, Canada, Argentina, and Australia also became major sellers of temperate agricultural products to Great Britain.

gentina that paved the way for participation in the new markets of Europe. One of these was the division of a vast area of the pampas into large landholdings, which were given to the military officers who had conquered the Indians and to others with influence in the government. Many of the smaller land-grant holders soon lost their land to neighbors with larger holdings.

Argentina thus acquired the latifundia system which is still in existence today. By 1914, farms with 2,500 acres or more accounted for 78.3 per cent of all land. In the Province of Buenos Aires, the richest grain- and meat-producing area, some 771 owners held 25 per cent of the land, whereas 23,000 small owners held only 20 per cent of the land. Substantial public lands existed only in the northeastern part of the country.

The distribution of land among a relatively small number of landholders facilitated the rapid development of the pampas, since these landowners had the means to fence off their holdings with the newly invented barbed wire and to bring in breeding cattle from abroad, principally from Great Britain. The number of cattle more than doubled between 1880 and 1900. Even more important, the quality of Argentine cattle improved greatly, since the native longhorn varieties were now crossed with the imported Durham, Shorthorn, and Hereford bulls. There was also a considerable expansion in the number and in the quality of the country's sheep.

Agricultural production also expanded greatly during the last two decades of the nineteenth century. The amount of cultivated land increased ten times; Argentina became a major exporter of wheat and also produced more maize and other crops than before.

As a direct result of the expansion of Argentina's agricultural capacities, a strong demand for labor arose. This demand was met principally by increased immigration, mainly from Italy and Spain. Many workers came only for the grain-harvesting season, but others stayed. Between 1880 and 1900, 1.3 million people migrated to Argentina.

During the last two decades of the nineteenth century, the railroad network grew rapidly, connecting Buenos Aires and other ports with the pampas. In 1880, the country possessed only 1,563 miles of railroad; by 1906, there were 12,274 miles. Sizable foreign capital, principally from Great Britain, was invested in the Argentine railway network, and for several generations its physical attributes resembled those of the British railways, since the stations, locomotives, and cars were either copied or imported from Great Britain. Two major ports were developed through which the products of the pampas were shipped to Europe. One was, of course, Buenos Aires. With the gradual perfection of packing techniques and refrigerated ships, Buenos Aires soon also became a meat-packing center. The large packing houses were mostly constructed by British and American firms.

The second major port was Rosario. Located on the northern edge of the pampas, Rosario handled the grains of the region, stored in huge silos in and near the city. In time, however, Rosario also became an important meat-packing and -shipping center.

Buenos Aires and Rosario handled not only cattle but also the sheep from Patagonia. Argentine mutton and lamb became as famous in Great Britain and on the Continent as Argentine beef.

These were not Argentina's only exports. Along the western edges of the pampas, near the city of Mendoza, where the great plain becomes dry, a prosperous wine industry developed, first for the domestic market, but later also for export to neighboring countries. In the north, in the provinces of Tucumán and Santiago del Estero, sugar growing, mostly for Argentine home consumption, was the most important economic occupation. (Sugar was produced on large plantations, and all efforts to unionize the workers failed until the advent of Perón. Labor conditions on the sugar plantations were therefore patriarchal and wretched.) In the northeastern section of the country, bordering on Paraguay, large plantations for the growing of yerba maté were developed. Scandals concerning special privileges given to yerba maté producers, as well as concerning labor conditions in the industry, occurred frequently during the period 1900–1940.

The Conservative Period

The Argentine economy developed further in the early twentieth century. Because of a growing grazing industry, more large packing-houses were built near Buenos Aires, owned largely by British and American firms. Also some small manufacturing plants developed in Buenos Aires and cities in the interior, particularly for the manufacture of textiles and shoes, light metallurgical products, and building materials. Most of these plants were established by immigrants who had begun their commercial careers in Argentina as merchants and craftsmen.

The development of railroads, modern ports, and small industries eventually led to the development of an organized labor movement. It began in the 1880's, and, by the early 1900's, there were two central labor organizations, the Federación Obrera Regional Argentina (FORA) and the Unión General de Trabajadores (UGT). FORA was of anarcho-syndicalist persuasion, while the UGT had a socialist leadership.

The first decade of the twentieth century was marked by substantial violence in labor relations. And this violence, and the issues that gave rise to it, reflected the increasingly unsatisfactory political situation. Democracy, as guaranteed by the constitution of 1853, was more theoretical than real. The government was firmly in the hands of the landed oligarchy, which was also the principal beneficiary of the country's economic development. The oligarchs' control was further strengthened by the fact that the secret ballot did not exist. Elections were often decided in the Casa Rosada, the presidential palace, before they even took place, by the simple expedient of the president and his advisers deciding whom they wanted to win in each province, and local officials then coercing the local electors to vote as they were told. Only in the city of Buenos Aires, where foreign observers could follow the electoral process, was there any semblance of free elections during this period.

Strong opposition to the political dominance of the rural oligarchy developed during the 1890's. It centered around two parties, the Unión Cívica Radical (UCR), or Radical Party, and the Socialist Party. The UCR was established in 1890 as the Unión Cívica by followers of ex-President Bartolomé Mitre, who attempted to topple the government and seize power by force. Although this effort failed, it did result in the resignation of President Juárez Celman.

Some of the younger and more militant members of Unión Cívica refused to accept former President Celman's vice-president as the new president and reorganized the Unión Cívica as the UCR. At first the UCR was headed by Leandro Alem and subsequently by Hipólito Irigoyen. It opposed all succeeding governments and, until 1912, refused to participate in any elections since their results were a foregone conclusion. On several occasions, the UCR attempted to incite military insurrections against the prevailing regime, but always failed.

The Socialist Party was also organized in the 1890's. Established mostly by immigrants, the party soon gained considerable influence among the working class of Buenos Aires. It elected its first member to the Chamber of Deputies, Alfredo Palacios, from the dock area of the city, in 1904. Because the Socialists were strong in Buenos Aires, where the chances for oppositionists to be victorious were greater than anywhere else, they were more willing than the UCR to take their chances with the electoral system.

The situation began to change with the election, in 1910, of President Roque Sáenz Peña. Although he represented the landed aristocracy, Sáenz Peña had strong democratic convictions. He felt that new electoral laws were needed to make the elections more representative of the choices of the voters. He pushed through Congress the so-called Sáenz Peña Law, which opened up a new period in Argentine political history.

The Sáenz Peña Law was unique. It provided for a secret ballot and also assured sufficient minority representation in the Congress. Specifically, the law stated that two-thirds of each province's representatives in the Chamber of Deputies should come from the party with the largest vote, and the remaining third should come from the second strongest party.

The Ascension of the Radicals

After the passage of the Sáenz Peña Law, the Radicals decided to participate in the elections. In 1914, they won a sizable representation in Congress and even a few governorships.

However, it was not until 1916 that the Radicals won their first national election, and that their leader, Hipólito Irigoyen, was elected president of the republic. But since Irigoyen did not have a majority in the Senate during most of his administration, he was not able to promote any significant legislation.

One of Irigoyen's characteristics as chief executive was that he tended to govern with a high hand, removing provincial governors who were his political opponents and even mistrusting his oldest and closest associates. A second aspect of the regime was the fact that by the time Irigoyen's party came to power it was also supported by some of the ruling economic groups, who opposed comparatively drastic reforms in labor legislation and other matters that Irigoyen was anxious to see enacted.

There was considerable labor unrest during the Irigoyen administration. In 1917, the workers won a major railroad strike. A walkout in a Buenos Aires metallurgical plant, in January, 1919, resulted in a general strike and several days of serious rioting, which ended only when President Irigoyen proclaimed martial law in the city. During the "Tragic Week," most of the city was in the hands of rioting mobs.

In 1922, the railroad workers established the Unión Ferroviaria, a labor organization that was to set the pattern for many others in future years. Indeed, it became the backbone of the Argentine labor movement. During the next two decades, the Unión Ferroviaria concentrated on collective bargaining with the employers and on developing an extensive network of social services for its members that was largely paid for by the railroads.

In 1922, the Radicals were again successful when Marcelo T. de Alvear, a Radical but also a member of the landed oligarchy, was elected president. Thereafter, the UCR split into two groups, the Anti-Personalist UCR, which backed President de Alvear, and the Personalist UCR, which supported ex-President Irigoyen. The tone of the de Alvear administration was generally conservative.

In 1928, Irigoyen ran again for the presidency and was elected. But by this time, he was almost eighty years old and trusted his colleagues infinitely less than he had during his first administration. In addition, the Radical administrations had by that time gained a reputation for being corrupt which, in turn, seriously undermined the prestige of the Irigoyen government. The only major piece of legislation it passed was a law establishing the Yacimientos Petrolíferos Fiscales, a government firm that was given the monopoly on the development of Argentina's petroleum resources. This measure ended almost a quarter of a century of agitation in favor of putting the country's oil reserves into the hands of Argentines and not foreigners.

The Great Depression, which began in 1929, brought the problems of the Irigoyen administration to a head since it critically reduced the volume of exports and cut down Argentina's ability to earn foreign currency. As a result, Argentina could no longer import the variety of goods to which its people were accustomed or pay its debts in foreign currency. The Irigoyen government developed no program to deal effectively with this serious economic crisis.

The Radicals thus lost their first significant opportunity to use the prosperity brought by the grain- and meat-exporting industries for encouraging industrialization and for developing an economy that was more diversified and less vulnerable to outside influences. It had also lost its chance to form a firm political union between the middle and urban and rural working classes, since it did not succeed in enacting the kind of labor and social legislation that would have given the lower classes full rights of citizenship.

It would be a mistake to judge the failure of the 1920's by the criteria of the 1960's. Given the history of the UCR and its close identification, before 1930, with the career of Irigoyen, it could not be expected that the UCR would play a leading role in Argentina's industrialization and social reform. The nationalist ideas of the Peruvian Victor Raúl Haya de la Torre, which were to provide the rationale for the demand of the middle and lower classes for social change and nationalistic economic development and which two decades later became the philosophy of many parties and political leaders in the hemisphere were still evolving. Economic nationalism, which gave a theoretical justification for industrialization and protectionism, as elaborated by Raúl Prebisch and his followers, was still a generation away. Argentine Radicalism under Irigoyen had few if any theoreticians; its speciality was practical politics.

With the failure of the Radicals during the period 1916–30, to provide middle-class civilian leadership, the UCR had lost its chance for leadership for at least a generation. The next attempt to unite the middle and working classes under a program of economic development and social reform was made by a military leader with dictatorial proclivities. This, however, was by no means clear in 1930.

The Conservative Reaction

The economic difficulties of the Irigoyen administration encouraged opponents of the regime to attempt its overthrow by force. Their efforts culminated in the ouster of the president by a military coup on September 6, 1930. This coup had the support not only of the leading military figures in Argentina but also of the Conservatives, the Anti-Personalist Radicals, and the Independent Socialists (who had broken away from the Socialist Party in 1928).

General José F. Uriburu became the provisional president of the new regime. During his two-year government, considerable confusion existed about the kind of government that the leaders of the coup wanted to impose. At first, there were plans for congressional and provincial elections in March, 1931. But when these elections were won by the UCR, the results were annulled, and the party was banned from further polls. Thereafter, Uriburu attempted to establish a corporative state, patterned after the Fascist regimes arising in Europe. However, military and civilian leaders, including army officers associated with the Anti-Personalist Radicals, opposed this development and forced Uriburu to desist and hold elections for president, for congress and state governors, and for legislatures in 1932. The Radicals were still banned from participation in the election and, through a combination of intimidation and corruption, government-backed candidates were generally assured of victory.

For the next eleven years, until June 4, 1943, the government was controlled by the military-civilian group that had seized power in 1930. The 1932 election was won by General Agustín P. Justo, a member of the Anti-Personalist UCR. In 1938, he was succeeded by another Anti-Personalist Radical, Dr. Roberto Ortiz. When Ortiz died two years later, Vice-President Ramón S. Castillo, a Conservative, assumed the presidency.

The men in power until 1943 maintained their control largely by force and corruption. Although the Radical and Socialist opposition controlled Congress during much of this time, these parties were never allowed to win a presidential election. They were prevented from doing so by outright and admitted fraud. Also, on several occasions, when the UCR or the equally oppositionist Progressive Democratic Party won control over provincial governments, the federal administration found excuses for removing the governors and calling new elections.

The regimes in power between 1932 and 1943 were strongly sympathetic to the landed interests. They were also particularly fearful of British retaliation against Argentine grain and meat exports if they made any move to protect Argentina's industry or to hamper British interests in Argentina. As a result, Argentina signed an agreement with Great Britain that protected British investments in Argentine public utilities. (One provision of this agreement affected Argentine-owned transportation facilities in Buenos Aires, and this outraged wide segments of Argentine public opinion.)

In spite of the anti-industrialization policies of the Argentine governments of the 1930's, industrialization moved ahead rapidly during this period, for the depression deprived Argentina of needed imports of manufactured goods.

Few Europeans immigrated during this period, and the workers for the new industries were recruited largely from the Argentine interior. These, however, were mostly agricultural workers who were not accustomed to industrial conditions, and they had no experience with trade unionism and little or no contact with radical political groups, such as anarchists, socialists, and Communists who had led the labor movement until that time. This was to be a decisive factor for Colonel Juan Domingo Perón's ascent to political power.

Only during the short period of Roberto Ortiz' presidency (1938–40) was there some modification of the Conservative pattern of the 1930's. Ortiz sought to end the anti-Radical interventions in various provinces, and showed considerable sympathy for the Allies at the outset of World War II. But with the death of Ortiz and accession of Ramón S. Castillo to power, the Argentine Government switched to a strongly "neutralist" stand on the war, although it showed considerable sympathy for European Fascist governments, particularly for Mussolini's Italy and Franco's Spain. Using the attack on Pearl Harbor as an excuse, the Castillo government decreed a state of siege—a modified form of martial law—which permitted it to limit a number of civil liberties.

The Perón Regime

In spite of his personal sympathies for the Axis powers, President Ramón S. Castillo was a loyal member of the conservative National Democratic Party. It was this fact which brought about his downfall.

Early in 1943, the party chose Robustiano Patrón Costas, a wealthy, pro-British landowner, as presidential candidate for the elections in 1944. But the principal leaders of the Argentine Army were strongly pro-Axis, and a long tradition of friendship existed with the German armed forces. (In the early decades of the twentieth century, there had been a German military mission in Argentina, and many of the leading officers had been trained in Nazi Germany.) Furthermore, the Argentine military then firmly expected that the Nazis would win the war, and they looked upon themselves as leaders of the pro-Axis elements in South America and, potentially, therefore, as a dominant force in the continent as a whole. Argentine Army leaders were thus strongly opposed to the election of a pro-British civilian president, and the prospect of this was the principal factor in bringing them to oust the government of Ramón S. Castillo, on June 4, 1943.

After a forty-eight-hour delay, General Pedro Ramírez, Castillo's Minister of Defense, was chosen as head of the new regime. He dissolved Congress and provincial legislatures, intervened in every province, and appointed military men to run them all. Ramírez also established a stringent censorship of the press and outlawed the principal pro-Allied organizations in Argentina. His government "intervened" in many civilian organizations and removed their leaders—which was unconstitutional. The most important organizations thus affected were the Unión Industrial Argentina, two railroad workers unions, the municipal workers union, and one faction of the General Federation of Labor, the Confederación General del Trabajo (CGT). A second faction of the CGT was outlawed, because of alleged Communist control.

These drastic steps turned most politically active Argentines against the new government. A group of younger military leaders soon came to the conclusion that the regime would have to win back civilian public opinion if it wanted to continue in power. These officers, of whom Colonel Juan Domingo Perón, Secretary to the Minister of War, was the most important, first turned to the industrialists and other middle-class groups for support. But these elements had traditionally backed the UCR and expected that it would in all likelihood come to power again. They saw no reason to compromise themselves, their party, or their expectations by making a deal with military men.

Rejected by the middle class, the young military men turned to organized labor. Since the first Irigoyen administration, no government had favored labor, and even Irigoyen had not succeeded in enacting any significant labor legislation. In 1943, because of growing labor unrest, the young military officers felt they had a chance to win working-class support if the government took an aggressively pro-labor position. In November, Colonel Perón was named Secretary of Labor and Social Welfare, and during the following two years he conducted a whirlwind campaign to build up a strong political base among the workers. The union leaders who were willing to work with him received his strong support for forcing recalcitrant employers to sign collective labor agreements. At the same time, Perón encouraged the formation of new unions among groups that had never been organized before, such as packing-house, sugar-plantation, and other agricultural workers. Finally, he enacted substantial labor and social measures by decree, including paid vacations, minimum wages, and an extensive social security system.

The political results of Perón's efforts soon became evident. By the middle of 1944, the CGT swung its support to Perón. At that time, he was Vice-President, Minister of War, and head of the Postwar Council, without having given up his post as Secretary of Labor.

The extent of Perón's working-class support became evident in October, 1945, when he was dismissed from all his government posts and jailed by an anti-Perón military group. A week of political confusion followed, during which Perón's working-class followers descended upon Buenos Aires and virtually seized control of the city. They met no resistance from the military, who could have suppressed Perón's supporters only at the cost of considerable bloodshed, a development they were unwilling to provoke. As a result, Perón was brought back to the presidential palace on October 16, 1945. The following day, he addressed a gigantic rally in the Plaza de Mayo, announcing, "I have returned."

Although Perón did not resume his old posts, he became a

presidential candidate in the February, 1946, elections. To back him, his labor followers formed the Labor Party. A dissident group of Radicals, reorganized as the Unión Cívica Radical Renovadora, and other miscellaneous groups, organized in the Independent Party, also supported Perón. All other political parties united against him. Most of them were organized in the coalition Unión Democratica, which named a Radical, José Tamborini, to run against Perón. The campaign was a hard-fought one (both candidates were shot at several times), but the voting was quiet and honest.

The 1946 presidential campaign reflected a lack of understanding by the opposition of the significance of the Peronista phenomenon. Significantly, the anti-Peronistas concentrated their attention on Perón's dictatorial and militaristic proclivities, dismissing as demagoguery the economic and social program that he had developed before and during the campaign. From a political point of view, it was a mistake that the Radicals and Socialists joined forces with the Conservatives against Perón and backed a courtly, stalwartly democratic gentleman of the old school, utterly lacking in social consciousness, to oppose Perón. There were elements within the UCR that opposed this coalition; but they were not sufficiently powerful to prevent a campaign that confirmed to large masses of Argentine workers that Perón was the only major politician who had their interests at heart.

Perón was elected with about 55 per cent of the vote. His followers nearly won a two-thirds majority in the Chamber of Deputies and gained all but two posts in the Senate. On June 4, 1946, Perón, by then a general, was inaugurated as president. He held this post for more than nine years.

Perón could have ruled as a democratic president if he had cared to do so. He had the support of a majority of the citizenry, and he began his administration with economic resources, which, if judiciously used, could have started Argentina on an exceedingly rapid process of economic development. However, although Perón did take important steps to diversify the economy, he made few efforts to establish a rational development program. Instead, the Perón government pushed forward an increasingly stringent dictatorship.

In the field of economics, Argentina had emerged from World War II with extensive foreign-exchange reserves in Great Britain and other countries that had purchased Argentine meat and grain during the war but had been unable to provide Argentina with manufactured goods in return. In addition, Argentine exports continued to be in great demand immediately following the war. Perón took advantage of these circumstances in several ways. Even before he was inaugurated, his government established the Instituto Argentino de Producción e Intercambio (IAPI), which was given the monopoly on selling Argentine meat abroad and in purchasing foreign manufactured goods. The foreign exchange generated through IAPI was used in various ways. Some was spent for importing heavy machinery and equipment for the country's booming industries. Other reserves were used to subsidize key consumer goods and keep down prices. Some funds went into the equipment of the Argentine armed forces; and other appreciable sums disappeared in the pockets of important figures in the Perón regime.

In contrast to its predecessors, the Perón government favored industry. In addition to providing industrialists with ample foreign exchange to import capital goods during the late 1940's, the government's Banco Industrial provided them with credits on reasonable terms. The government also established a system of relatively high protective tariffs. This support of industrialization was but one aspect of Perón's emphasis on nationalism. Another part of his program was designed to repatriate foreign investments in Argentina; however, this effort was widely criticized by economists at home and abroad. The most important action in this field was the purchase, in 1948, of the British-owned Argentine railroads, for which the Perón government spent the value of one year's meat exports to Britain.

By the early 1950's, however, Argentina had used up its accumulated foreign-exchange reserves and the country faced a growing economic crisis. Inflation became so serious that, by the time Perón was overthrown, it had virtually wiped out the real wage gains the Argentine workers had achieved during the first five years of the Perón era.

The crisis was further intensified by the decline in Argentine agriculture. This decline had begun before Perón came to power but grew more serious under his rule, since Perón put a serious squeeze on the country's grazers and agriculturalists. On the one hand, IAPI paid abnormally low prices to the producers of export commodities when world prices for these products were abnormally high; on the other, Perón's labor program, which unionized the agricultural workers and provided them with protective laws, exerted severe upward pressure on the costs of production.

The rural situation in the early 1950's was further complicated by serious droughts, so that Argentina could not meet its export commitments for cattle and grain. In 1952, Argentina was forced to import grain from Romania and the United States.

Perón was not unaware of the country's growing economic difficulties, and his second Five-Year-Plan, which began in 1952, laid particular stress on the recuperation of agriculture. These efforts showed only modest results, however, and by 1955 the country was still suffering from serious inflation and agriculture had by no means recovered.

Meanwhile, Perón's regime had become increasingly dictatorial. A thorough purge of the labor movement, directed by Perón's wife, Eva Duarte de Perón (Evita), removed virtually all union leaders in office when Perón came to power. They were the men who had helped Perón; but since they had a power base of their own and did not owe their offices to Perón and his wife, they were dangerous in the eyes of the regime. Evita replaced them with men who had a debt to the President and the first lady.

In 1949, Perón authorized a constitutional assembly to write a new constitution. In addition to writing some of Perón's social and economic ideas into the new document, this assembly greatly increased the power of the president and included a new provision that allowed the re-election of the president and vice-president.

Freedom of the press was destroyed by a variety of stratagems. Some newspaper owners were forced to sell out to a chain of publications controlled by Evita. Others were closed down because they were suddenly discovered to have violated the public-health code or some other irrelevant legislation. Hundreds of periodicals were discontinued on the grounds that they disobeyed an order of the government that all publications carry the slogan "Year of the Liberator San Martín" in 1950, the year of the hundredth anniversary of the Liberator's death—an order that was issued only after the papers had been closed down for "evading" it.

The same tactics were used against opposition political parties. Their headquarters were closely watched by the police and their leaders frequently jailed on a variety of often petty charges. Many political leaders were forced into exile. Others went into hiding to avoid being picked up by the police. Laws were passed that prevented the formation of united opposition slates against the Peronistas; the election districts were gerrymandered so as to assure the Peronistas—who were in the majority in any case—of an overwhelming control over the Congress and the provincial legislatures.

During its last years, the Perón administration seemed to strive toward the establishment of some kind of a corporative state, and it attempted to establish organizations among employers, professional groups, and university students that paralleled the thoroughly cowed CGT. To this end, the Confederación General Económica (CGE) was established for employers in agriculture, industry, and commerce, the Confederación General de Profesionales for the members of the free professions, and the Confederación General Universitaria (CGU) was set up to control the university students, whose Federación Universitaria Argentina carried on an unremitting struggle against the regime. Of these three groups, only the CGE was able to enlist an appreciable number of members.

Throughout his regime, Perón's power rested principally on the labor movement and the armed forces. After 1949, the leadership of the CGT and of its constituent unions was named by Evita Perón, and after her death, in 1952, by the Minister of Labor, presumably in consultation with Perón. The armed forces were kept in line by a combination of frequent command changes, ample funds, and an efficient espionage system covering the activities of most military leaders.

Perón at first enjoyed the support of the Catholic Church. In the 1946 presidential election, the bishops issued a pastoral letter endorsing his candidacy, priests were active in Perón's political party, and most members of the hierarchy were ostentatiously friendly to his regime during its early years.

In the early 1950's, however, relations noticeably cooled between Perón and Church leaders. By 1954, open hostility existed between the regime and the Church hierarchy. Churches were burned by Perón supporters, priests were arrested, and some were even deported. The government repealed the 1944 decree establishing Catholic teaching in public schools and passed laws to legalize divorce and prostitution.

The open conflict between the Perón regime and the Church contributed to the eventual overthrow of the dictatorship, for many of Perón's working-class supporters who were also good Catholics were disconcerted by the conflict. Many military men who had previously been either favorable to Perón or at least neutral turned against the regime for the same reason.

Provisional Governments After Perón

An attempt by the navy and air force to overthrow Perón in June, 1955, failed. However, a second coup, in September, 1955, which had the backing not only of the navy and of most of the air force but also of significant elements of the army and numerous civilians armed by the rebellious military, succeeded. With the triumph of the revolt against him, Perón went into exile. Going first to Paraguay, he later sought refuge in Venezuela, Panama, the Dominican Republic, and ultimately in Spain.

Perón's immediate successor was General Eduardo Lonardi, who had led the revolt in Córdoba. His regime, however, did not take any definite direction. It sought to conciliate the defeated Peronistas by raising the slogan "Neither victor nor vanquished," and, although Lonardi outlawed the Peronista Party, he allowed Peronistas to remain in control of the labor movement. But the new government was soon riven by a conflict between leaders of the traditional political parties on the one hand and elements of the extreme Catholic Right and some ex-Peronistas who had turned against the dictator in the early 1950's on the other. Lonardi was ousted after two months by General Pedro Eugenio Aramburu. (Lonardi's vice-president, Admiral Isaac Rojas, continued in office.) The Aramburu-Rojas regime was unequivocally anti-Peronista. Facing a general strike called by the Peronistas, it removed the leadership of the CGT and most of its constituent unions and replaced them with military officers. It also arrested many Peronista ex-legislators and trade-union officials and held them without formal charges. When the Peronistas attempted a countercoup on

June 9, 1956, the regime responded violently. For the first time since the days of Rosas, military and civilian leaders of a coup against the government were executed.

The Aramburu regime took steps to liberalize the economy. IAPI was dissolved, and it was announced that the government intended to abandon its monopoly of the export-import trade. The CGE, CGP, and CGU were also dissolved, and the government reverted to a policy favoring agriculture rather than industry.

During the two and a half years of the Aramburu administration, most workers reverted to their loyalty to Perón. Many workers had been disillusioned with Perón, but the actions of the Aramburu government, whose military officers controlled the CGT for a long time and which filled key positions in the Ministry of Labor with industrial management personnel, convinced many that the government was opposed to the working class and that their only real friend was the deposed dictator.

Aramburu's principal accomplishment was the restoration of constitutional government. Soon after coming to power, he suspended the Peronista constitution of 1949 and reinstated the constitution of 1853. Subsequently, he called elections for a constituent assembly to discuss major changes in the constitution, but this body was unable to reach agreement.

In February, 1958, elections were held for president, vice-president, provincial governors and legislators, the federal Senate, and the Chamber of Deputies. The two major candidates in this election represented rival factions of the UCR (which had split, late in 1956, into the Unión Cívica Radical Intransigente and the Unión Cívica Radical del Pueblo). The nominee of the Intransigente faction was Arturo Frondizi, who had been president of the UCR before its split. His rival was Ricardo Balbín, who had been the Radicals' candidate for president in the election of 1951 that was won by Perón.

The Peronistas, who were not allowed to organize into a party of their own and who had boycotted the 1957 election for a constituent assembly, followed Perón's instructions from abroad and voted for Frondizi. They thus assured Frondizi of a sufficiently large majority so that the military, which might have been inclined to prevent Frondizi from taking office, felt that it was in no position to do so.

The Frondizi Regime

Arturo Frondizi's political prominence began after he had been elected to the Chamber of Deputies, in 1946. He headed the "Young Turk" faction in the UCR, which claimed to be heir of the Irigoyen tradition, and he opposed the increasingly conservative attitude of the party after the advent of Perón. Frondizi and his fellow Intransigentes maintained that it was foolish to oppose everything Perón did just because Perón did it. They argued that it was necessary to recognize the important changes Perón had brought about, such as an expanded labor movement and the enactment of long-overdue social legislation, and that the Radicals should make it clear they were opposed not to these measures but only to his dictatorship.

In the early 1950's, Frondizi was elected president of the UCR. As such, he tended to operate in a somewhat high-handed fashion, reorganizing the party in provinces where his opponents were predominant, and thereby annoying many of the older party leaders. Quite contrary to UCR tradition, he gathered an outstanding group of young intellectuals around him who sought to work out a program that the party could follow if and when it came to power. Gradually, he became convinced that only a major effort to develop the economy, particularly industry, and the reintegration of the Peronistas into the political life of the nation could end Argentina's stagnation and frustration. When he became president, Frondizi's two major problems were the threat of unrestrained inflation undermining any development efforts and the fact that the military leaders were fundamentally distrustful of him, suspecting him of Peronista or even Communist leanings.

In an attempt to deal with the first of these problems, Frondizi adopted a stringent price-stabilization policy, which involved the limitation of wage increases, selective credit controls, and an attempt to balance the federal budget. At the same time, he sought to encourage large-scale investment by both domestic and foreign entrepreneurs. Therefore, he modified the old Irigoyen policy of government monopoly in the petroleum industry and ordered the YPF to sign a series of contracts with foreign oil companies to explore for and exploit oil in various parts of the country. He also settled several other vexing foreign-investment problems, particularly in public utilities. The terms of settlement were usually quite favorable to the foreign interests but had the effect of attracting considerable foreign investments. Frondizi also used credit controls, tariff policy, and other measures to encourage new investment. As a result, significant advances were made in petrochemical manufacturing, the automobile industry, and other key sectors of the national economy.

By early 1962, Frondizi's economic-stabilization and development program had begun to bear fruit. The international exchange value of the Argentine peso had been stabilized, and price increases had almost been brought under control. Argentina had been converted from a major importer to a net exporter of petroleum. Various new industries were being established.

Frondizi's economic program had aroused widespread opposition, however, among workers, whose wages were held in check; entrepreneurs, whose requests for credit were not considered essential; and railroad workers, who felt menaced by government attempts to rationalize the operation of the lines.

In late 1961, it became clear that other groups were also joining the opposition. The nationalists were outraged because the government opened the petroleum industry to foreign firms; anticlericals were annoyed because Frondizi sponsored legislation for the establishment of Catholic universities.

In March, 1962, the opponents of President Frondizi got a chance to voice their misgivings, for at that time he set about to achieve the other basic objective of his regime—the reintegration of the Peronistas into Argentina's political life. Frondizi had first hoped for an amalgamation of the Peronistas, his own Intransigentes, and various smaller groups in a united movement. This, however, failed, and the Peronistas were then allowed to organize their own parties in most provinces. These parties participated in the elections of late 1961 and January, 1962, but won only a few positions. In March, 1962, however, the Peronistas won strong victories in the gubernatorial elections in ten provinces and, throughout the country, for members of the Chamber of Deputies. The leaders of the Argentine armed forces now took fright. Even those who had previously opposed any move to overthrow the government joined forces with the enemies of the regime. The President was deposed, and the president of the Senate, José María Guido, took his place.

Guido and Illia

For the next fifteen months, the economic and political situation in Argentina was chaotic. The international value of the Argentine peso plummeted, inflation picked up speed once again, Frondizi's investment program was curtailed, and capital fled the country. The Guido government itself was a faintly disguised military dictatorship, characterized by bitter fights among contending factions.

The conflicting military groups were known as the Colorados ("Reds") and the Azules ("Blues"). The Colorados favored outright military dictatorship, of indefinite duration, which would liquidate the Peronistas. The Azules favored a return to constitutional government by elections and a compromise with the Peronistas. In September, 1962, the two groups clashed in a short civil war, in which the Azules emerged victorious under the leadership of General Juan Carlos Onganía.

Elections were, in fact, held in June, 1963. They, too, were chaotic. The Unión Cívica Radical del Pueblo named Arturo Illia, a provincial doctor and old-time politician, as its candidate for president. A large section of the Intransigentes broke with Frondizi and named its own candidate, Dr. Oscar Alende. Frondizi himself joined forces with the followers of Perón in a Movement of Popular Unity. The electoral authorities vetoed three presidential nominees of the Movement, however, and, both Perón (from abroad) and Frondizi ended the impasse by urging the voters to cast blank ballots. Several other minor party candidates also ran. Arturo Illia was elected, although he had received only one-quarter of the vote. Illia's victory brought a profound sense of relief to the populace, and, for a few months, his mild-mannered government gained widespread popular support among both civilians and the military. However, as time passed, it became obvious that Illia's way of dealing with the country's major problems was to avoid taking any decisive action. (One of the few actions the Illia government did take damaged the Argentine economy considerably: This was the cancellation of the contracts that the Frondizi government had made with various foreign oil companies and the return of the oil industry to the YPF. As a result, Argentina soon had to import petroleum products again and was faced with having to find a solution to a lingering international issue that was very difficult to resolve.) Opposition to his regime began to mount.

In conformity with the line of the "Blues" in 1962–63 and

with President Illia's own inclinations, the government allowed the Peronistas to maintain provincial parties with no ostensible ties among them. However, a national leadership, under close direction of the exiled Juan Domingo Perón, continued to exist. When a group of Peronistas led by Augusto Vandor of the Metallurgical Union sought, late in 1965, to establish a separate legal party, Perón opposed this move, apparently fearful that such a group might develop a leadership that would be beyond his control. A major split in the Peronista ranks developed.

In spite of it, however, many Argentines feared that the Peronistas would win in ten provinces (including the two largest, Buenos Aires and Santa Fé) in the elections scheduled for March, 1967. This fear, and the ineptitude of the Illia government, provoked still another military coup, in June, 1966.

The new president was General Juan Carlos Onganía. Now favoring the Colorados' program he had opposed so long, Onganía made it clear that he and the military men associated with him intended to stay in power for a long time, perhaps ten years. Onganía—in a series of moves that had many precedents in Argentine history—dissolved Congress and the provincial legislatures, appointed military men to run all of the provincial governments, replaced all members of the Supreme Court, and abolished all existing political parties. Thus, the political crises that had plagued Argentina since the seizure of power by the military in 1930 continued. It seemed unlikely that it would be resolved so long as there remained any possibility that Perón might return to power.

III

The Economy

A major element of Argentina's continuing crisis is its ailing economy. Although the export-based economy that had developed by the beginning of World War I was able to provide high levels of living for the country's residents, it suffered from grave weaknesses. Its ability to expand was limited, and it made Argentina dangerously dependent on outside influences over which the country had little control. Most important, Argentina was unable to build a more rounded and more broadly based economy upon its early but precarious prosperity.

One of the fundamental reasons for Argentina's failure to develop a diversified economy, and particularly to stimulate manufacturing industries, has been the long-continuing conviction of large segments of public opinion that Argentina is "naturally" a grazing-agricultural nation. A corollary to this belief is the opinion that governmental protection for manufacturing is unjustified, and, further, that it might endanger the prosperity of the rural economy.

This opposition to protectionism and, in turn, the general support for free trade were professed by diverse political groups. Even Juan B. Justo, the founder of the Argentine Socialist Party, was a long-time advocate of free trade. Only the Irigoyen wing of the Radical Party (UCR), and its ideological successor, the Intransigentes of the Perón and post-Perón periods, were strong advocates of industrialization, although Hipólito Irigoyen did nothing to enact a program of protectionism when he was president from 1916 to 1922 and from 1928 to 1930.

Another major factor contributing to and drawing strength from the anti-protectionist inclinations of Argentine public opinion was the strong resistance to protectionism by the large landowning group that dominated Argentina's export-based economy. The landholders who raised the cattle and grew the grain that was shipped abroad greatly feared that their trading partners, particularly Great Britain, might retaliate if Argentina attempted to protect industries that produced goods traditionally imported from Europe. They used all their political influence to fight the protectionist sentiment and were particularly successful in determining government policy during the 1930's.

A third major factor hampering development of industrialization was the vacillation in government policy over several decades. Starting in 1943, the Perón regime was favorable toward manufacturing, but its enthusiasm declined in the early 1950's. The Aramburu government was not friendly toward industry, the Frondizi regime favored industry again, and the post-Frondizi governments have generally been equivocal on the subject.

There were other extraneous factors that handicapped the elaboration of a proper economic-development policy. One was Juan Domingo Perón himself. His support of industrialization tended to make such a program suspect among sizable elements of the Argentine political community which might otherwise have supported it. Another was inflation, which has racked the economy for almost two decades and which has often seemed to demand policies antagonistic to industrialization.

To understand fully the economic aspects of the Argentine crisis, it is important to trace their development since 1930, when Argentina slipped more or less rapidly from its economic eminence among the countries of Latin America. At least five periods are clearly discernible since 1930: the years 1930–43; the Perón period, 1943–55; the years of the *Revolución Libertadora* ("Liberating Revolution"), 1955–58; the Frondizi epoch, 1958–62; and the period since President Arturo Frondizi's overthrow in March, 1962.

Characteristics of an Export-based Economy

Grazing and agriculture have long given Argentina the highest level of living in Latin America. Although figures indicate that Argentina's per-capita income in 1960 ($505) was second in Latin America only to that of Venezuela ($1,120), Argentine earnings were more evenly distributed than Venezuelan income, with the result that the average Argentine was materially much better off than his Venezuelan counterpart.

For many decades, Argentina has had a larger middle class than any Latin American country; perhaps half of the population belongs to that category. Although, like other nations of the area, Argentina has miserable slums of shanties ringing its major cities, with jerry-built houses made out of packing boxes and other castaway materials, only a relatively small proportion of the total population of Buenos Aires and of other urban centers live there. And although there are some segments of the rural population—particularly in the north—that live in conditions comparable to the semifeudal circumstances in other Latin American countries, most of the laborers on the large *estancias* of the pampas have since the Perón period enjoyed working and living conditions much better than those in most other Latin American countries.

The Argentines generally eat better than most Latin Americans. Their average caloric intake is 3,360 calories. No other Latin American nation approaches this level which is even superior to the 3,100 calories in the United States and 3,070 in Canada. The Argentines are among the world's greatest meat eaters, consuming about 257 pounds per person a year, compared with about 238 pounds eaten in Uruguay, the Western Hemisphere's second largest meat-consuming country. Bread, pasta, and other grain products, as well as vegetables, fruits, and wine are also consumed in large quantities.

Despite the deterioration of the housing situation in recent decades, Argentines, particularly those living in the cities, still live in considerably better conditions than virtually all other Latin Americans. Argentina's literacy rate of around 90 per cent is rivaled, in Latin America, only by Uruguay and perhaps Costa Rica.

The country has a fairly modern system of taxation. Until the 1930's, Argentine public finances depended largely on customs revenues. However, as a result of the Great Depression, the revenue from import taxes declined dramatically, and the government of General Agustín P. Justo was the first to introduce the income tax. In subsequent years, the income tax has provided an increasingly large portion of the government's income.

The advent of the Great Depression found Argentina in a position calling for the development of a more diversified and self-sufficient economy, and the country's tragedy since that time has been the failure to develop a new and more rounded economic life. The Great Depression dramatically uncovered the first serious weakness of the Argentine economy, namely, its excessive dependence on a narrow range of export products. In his history of the Bank of London and South America, David Joslin has well summarized the nature of this weakness:

> the future of the River Plate Republics depended on a limited range of exports which were highly sensitive to changes in world markets. Argentina and Uruguay were debtor countries with fixed interest payments to make abroad. Their ranchers and farmers had to export to live, and so earnings were kept as

high as possible by increasing sales when prices fell. An early warning of changing circumstances came in June 1929, when gold began to be drained from Argentina to New York and London. Bank deposits began to sag in September, and in December the convertibility of the Argentine peso was suspended.

Later on, Joslin adds:

Meagre grain harvests and falling grain prices placed pressure on the Argentine exchanges, no longer buttressed by an influx of foreign capital. . . . Falling exchange rates increased the price of imports and added 20 per cent to the cost of servicing the foreign debt. Depression bred commercial uneasiness and political discontent . . .*

The very nature of Argentina's previous prosperity made the impact of falling grain and meat prices and sales even more catastrophic than might have been the case with another kind of economy. Grazing and grain production had brought the great majority of the Argentines into the market and had accustomed them to using imported manufactured goods that had been bought with the proceeds from the country's exports. As a result, and contrary to the situation in a country where large segments of the population were still engaged in subsistence agriculture and thus relatively unaffected by what happened in the commercial sectors of the economy, most Argentines suffered from the collapse of Argentina's exports. Incomes fell throughout the economy, and people of all classes were unable to obtain the goods they had become accustomed to buying.

In the 1930's, it became clear the nature of Argentine economy could subject the country to pressure from abroad. When the British Empire and Commonwealth established a system of tariff preferences for its members at the Ottawa Conference of 1932, Argentine exporters were frightened that their meat and grain would be excluded from their

* David Joslin, *A Century of Banking in Latin America* (New York: Oxford University Press, 1963), pp. 246 and 248.

principal market in Great Britain in favor of exports from Canada, Australia, and New Zealand. As a result, the Argentine governments, which were dominated in the 1930's and early 1940's by the rural landholding interests, were willing to agree to almost any British demand as price for keeping the British market open to Argentine products. They were therefore hostile to industrialization, fearing that any protection given Argentine manufacturing would provoke British retaliation and would be advantageous to Argentina's competitors. Specifically, the government of President Agustín P. Justo signed an agreement with Great Britain in 1935, giving British businessmen in Argentina special concessions that were widely regarded as not only injurious to Argentine entrepreneurs but also as denigrating of the national sovereignty.

The final weakness of the Argentine economy, its inability to grow much further along the lines followed between 1860 and 1930, would even have been clear had the Great Depression never occurred. Argentina already had as much of the British market for grains and meat as it could ever hope to achieve. Other European countries bought smaller amounts of Argentine products but were generally interested in developing their own internal supply sources or were already self-sufficient in the products that Argentina exported. The United States was not a likely market, because it not only produced similar products for its own consumption but also had large exportable surpluses. Finally, the grain and meat production of Canada, Australia, New Zealand, and other countries was challenging Argentine superiority even before the Depression.

If Argentina's economy was to expand further, it had to develop in different directions. Manufacturing, that is, the production of industrial goods for the internal market and for possible export to some of Argentina's neighbors, was one of the most likely directions of development. However, as we have noted, this trend was hampered by the essentially anti-industrial philosophy of all governments before 1943.

Industrialization and Foreign-Exchange Problems

And yet, manufacturing had developed on a modest scale before 1943. Even during World War I, there was a sufficient internal market to support a considerable number of small-scale factories and workshops. In 1914, as much as 37 per cent of all processed foods consumed in the country, as well as 17 per cent of the clothing and 12 per cent of the metal goods, was produced at home. In the ensuing years, manufacturing increased to the point where industry passed agriculture in terms of its contribution to the gross national product after World War II, the former providing 24 per cent and the latter only 19 per cent. This industrial development had occurred largely despite the Argentine Government, due to causes over which the Argentines in general had little or no control.

The Great Depression, beginning in 1929, provided a kind of automatic protection for new manufacturing industries in Argentina. Because the country had great difficulty in selling its grain and meat at good prices on the world market, it did not earn the foreign exchange it had customarily received in previous decades. Not only was Argentina thus unable to import the usual quantities of manufactured goods from Europe, but the drastic devaluation of the Argentine peso during this period made imported goods more expensive than before.

The result of this situation was that many Argentine entrepreneurs soon found out that it was possible for them to establish new enterprises that were not faced with serious competition from abroad, and the woolen textile industry, food-processing firms, and light metallurgical enterprises expanded rapidly during the Great Depression.

World War II intensified this situation. Argentina continued to sell its agricultural and grazing products to Great Britain, where they were in great demand, but the British were unable to return manufactured goods as a result of the war. Argentina, therefore, accumulated in Great Britain, and to a less degree in the United States, a sizable foreign-exchange balance, which it could not use to pay for imports, at least until after World War II.

These factors favoring industrialization were supplemented by a change in government policy when Perón came to power. Not only did Perón favor the development of manufacturing and was generally hostile to the country's traditional grazing and agricultural economy, he also took a number of measures to encourage the growth of industry during his ten years in power. One of the major instruments of Perón's economic policy was the Instituto Argentino de Promoción del Intercambio (IAPI). Through it, the government bought up virtually all of the country's meat production and subsequently also most of its grain output. For several years, these products were sold within Argentina at low prices so as to prevent inflation. The remainder was sold abroad by the IAPI at whatever prices the world market would bear. However, since IAPI paid grazers and agriculturalists much less than world-market prices, it provided the government with a handy profit, which the government, in turn, used for a variety of purposes.

A sizable part of the profit of IAPI was spent for equipment for the country's enlarged armed forces, and some of it went to line the pockets of insiders of the regime; nevertheless, a portion of the proceeds from the sale of meat and grain abroad was used to repatriate foreign investments in Argentine railroads and other enterprises, and a considerable share was made available to the nation's industrialists. Particularly during the late 1940's, the Perón government followed a very liberal policy of making available scarce foreign exchange, so that manufacturers could import needed machinery and other equipment.

The Perón government also supplemented the foreign exchange invested in industry with peso loans. For this purpose, the regime established the Banco Industrial, whose main purpose was to finance the growth of the country's manufacturing with pesos. A reversal of the country's tariff policies accompanied this direct aid to manufacturing. The government initiated a high protectionist policy. As a result, when European and American manufactured goods would normally have begun to stream back into the country (particularly in the early 1950's), Argentine industrialists were protected by a tariff wall.

The government also undertook to establish some industrial enterprises. The four most important were a steel plant, constructed under the direction of the Ministry of Defense in the Buenos Aires provincial city of San Nicolás; the nation's first large-scale automobile enterprise, established in conjunction with the Kaiser firm of the United States, in the city of Córdoba; and two smaller firms, also in Córdoba, an airplane factory and an agricultural implement firm, in which the government cooperated with the Italian Fiat company.

Finally, the agricultural policies followed by the Perón regime served to stimulate industry as well. IAPI tended to keep agricultural prices low, while Perón's labor policies raised wages, established rural trade unions, and included agricultural workers in the social-security system, all of which raised the labor costs in agriculture. Thus, the *estancia* owners were caught in a predicament: They received low prices for their products, but had to pay high costs for production. The result was that now a few landholders found it more profitable to withdraw some of their capital from agriculture and to invest it in manufacturing.

In its later years, however, the Perón government ran into serious difficulties with its industrialization program. The most serious problem was the shortage of foreign exchange. Partly because of the IAPI policy of paying very low prices to the grazers and agriculturalists, the area of land under both grain production and cattle feeding declined drastically. Although the tendency toward economic decline antedated the advent of the Perón regime, it was certainly greatly intensified by Peronista policies.

Two other factors intensified the country's foreign-exchange difficulties in the early 1950's. First, there was a series of droughts that killed many cattle and kept agricultural production low. Second, the Argentines were now consuming an increasing proportion of their own meat and wheat output. The population was growing, albeit relatively slowly, and during the late 1940's, real wages had risen considerably. As a result, an increasingly large proportion of the country's meat and wheat production was destined for the internal market. The situation reached crisis proportions in 1952. At that time, Argentina could no longer meet its commitments to sell meat and wheat abroad, and the country was actually forced to import some grain from Romania and the United States. Meatless days were instituted, and the quality and quantity of bread, pasta, and other wheat products dropped drastically.

To a very small degree, the Perón regime was able to offset its foreign-exchange difficulties by borrowing from abroad and by enticing some private foreign investment to enter the country. Thus, Argentina received a loan of $125,000,000 from the Export-Import Bank in 1950 for financing the first stages of the San Nicolás steel plant. It was also possible to get the Fiat and Kaiser companies to join the government in the industrial projects already mentioned and to get the Standard Oil Company of California to agree to help exploit the country's oil reserves.

However, the jingoistic and even xenophobic nationalism which had characterized Perón's policies and speeches during the early years of his administration made both private foreign investors and intergovernmental lending institutions wary about coming into Argentina. Furthermore, Perón's sudden switch to a policy of accepting international loans and encouraging foreign investment aroused opposition among his followers. Thus, the usually compliant Congress procrastinated about approving the arrangement which Perón had made with the Standard Oil Company of California. When the Perón regime was overthrown, in September, 1955, the agreement had still not been signed.

The governments of the *revolución libertadora,* which immediately succeeded Perón largely reversed his economic policies. Once again, the regime was highly favorable to agriculture and grazing. The Aramburu administration dissolved IAPI, began to phase the government out of the grain and meat business, and provided the agriculturalists and grazers with much higher prices than Perón had offered them. Between 1955 and 1958, the government gave little encouragement to industry.

The Frondizi Program and After

With the advent of Arturo Frondizi to the presidency, in May, 1958, the Argentine Government once again reverted to a policy that favored industry and attempted at the same time to encourage agricultural diversification. Frondizi rejected the idea that industry and agriculture are mutually exclusive.

The Frondizi government was faced with several major economic problems. First, the inflation that had begun during Perón's administration and had continued during his successors' regimes threatened to get completely out of control during the first months of the Frondizi administration, partly because Frondizi had to pay off his election promises of large wage increases. Second, Frondizi felt that it was necessary to reverse the process of decapitalization of much of the nation's economy that had been going on since the Great Depression and was characterized by the deterioration of the country's railroads, roads, and public utilities. Third, the Frondizi regime felt that it was necessary to provide the country with a more diversified pattern of agricultural exports and, if possible, to supplement this with some nonagricultural export products. Fourth, Frondizi wanted to come to grips with the country's growing deficit in petroleum products, and, finally, he wished to set the country on a path of rapid industrialization.

During the four years that the Frondizi regime was allowed by the military to stay in power, it largely achieved these objectives. Through a program of austerity, which was launched late in 1958 and was characterized by selective credit controls, limitation of wage increases, foreign-exchange controls, and an attempt to bring the federal budget closer to a balance, the rate of inflation was greatly slowed down, and the international exchange rate of the peso was stabilized during the second half of Frondizi's administration.

The government drew up a program for rationalizing the operation of the railroads and for improving their equipment. Frondizi overcame stubborn trade-union resistance to the scaling down of railroad employment and received some foreign help for bringing in new rolling stock and for improving other aspects of the railway system. A large highway building and improvement program was also started, for which about $95 million was provided, $48.5 million coming from a loan received from the International Bank for Reconstruction and Development (IBRD).

Progress was also made in trying to halt the deterioration of the country's public utilities. Under Perón and Aramburu, the foreign companies that provided most of the country's gas and electricity had been expropriated, but no terms of settlement had been reached with these enterprises. Frondizi settled both with the Belgian-Spanish firm that provided most of the power and gas for greater Buenos Aires and with the American and Foreign Power Company, which handled most public utilities in the interior of the country. In the case of Buenos Aires, a new mixed company, partly government owned, partly belonging to the foreign concessionaire, was organized. The concessionaire agreed to invest $109 million toward a $292 million expansion program, and an IBRD loan of $95 million was also received. Somewhat similar arrangements were made with the American and Foreign Power Company.

The agricultural program of the Frondizi government was principally designed to encourage the growth of more corn and small grains and of less wheat. The theory behind this program was that world wheat markets tended to be glutted, whereas there was ample room for the expansion of Argentine corn and other grain exports. However, only modest success was achieved with this policy.

To deal with the growing petroleum shortage—which resulted in the country's spending approximately $300 million a year to import oil, an amount just about equal to the deficit in Argentina's balance of payments—Frondizi took the highly unpopular measure of allowing foreign firms to come into the country's oil industry on a massive scale. Ever since the late 1920's, it had been government policy to put the major burden of providing for the nation's oil needs upon the government-owned Yacimientos Petrolíferos Fiscales (YPF), and Perón's attempt to alter this policy had substantially contributed to his downfall.

Perhaps the same was true of Frondizi. The Frondizi government enacted a new petroleum law, which totally nationalized the country's oil reserves but allowed the government and YPF to enter into contracts—the word "concessions" was carefully avoided—with private companies, foreign or domestic, to help discover oil and to get it out of the ground. In each case, the foreign firm was to act as an agent of YPF and was to sell the oil to the YPF if YPF so desired. The foreign companies were given title neither to the land under which the oil was found nor to the petroleum that might be discovered.

The results of this new policy were spectacular. By the time Frondizi was overthrown, the country had been converted from a major importer of petroleum to a net exporter. Although Argentina still imported some specialized types of petroleum products, it also exported considerable amounts of crude oil, worth more than the processed products the country still imported.

The Frondizi regime also took major steps toward further industrialization and initiated a program for considerably expanding the San Nicolás steel plant. Foreign firms were encouraged to come to Argentina and to establish a full-scale integrated automobile industry; they were in the process of doing so before Frondizi was ousted. A large U.S. combine joined with the Argentine Government to establish a huge petrochemical enterprise. The construction of this company was begun by the end of the Frondizi period, and many smaller domestic and foreign industrial enterprises followed.

Had Frondizi been allowed to remain in office, he almost certainly would have been able to put an end to the stagnation of the Argentine economy, which the country had been suffering for more than a decade. However, his overthrow points to one of the major reasons why this stagnation has continued: No government has been able to implement for a sufficiently long time a program of general economic development such as Perón had in the late 1940's and Frondizi in the period 1958–62. Economic development, and particularly industrialization, has never become a generally accepted basic objective of government policy in Argentina, and the attitudes toward development have tended to shift with each succeeding regime.

Those governments that came after Frondizi allowed most of his programs to disintegrate. Although the post-Frondizi governments continued the industrialization projects already under way, few new ones were undertaken. The Illia government canceled all oil contracts negotiated by Frondizi, and Argentina once again became a major oil-importing country. The regime that succeeded Illia reversed this policy once again by allowing foreign participation in the country's oil development. It is still too early to know what the long-term effects of this latest change will be. Also Frondizi's efforts to reorganize the railroads were largely abandoned, though his attempts to expand and improve the public utilities were continued but not expanded. The general air of insecurity that has existed in the years since Arturo Frondizi's overthrow in March, 1962, has made both foreign and domestic entrepreneurs leary of making further heavy investments. Similarly, little constructive use has been made of Argentina's foreign credit to further economic development since 1962.

As a result of the instability of government and the frequent changes of official economic policy during the post-Frondizi period, the Argentine economy has behaved very spottily. Industrial production, for instance, rose 14.1 per cent in 1964—almost equal to the best year of the Frondizi period—but then fell back to 11.1 per cent in 1965 and declined by an additional 1.4 per cent in 1966, the year of the Onganía coup. The Onganía government, which came to power in June, 1966, seemed to turn its back once again on industrialization and, in the name of providing lower prices for the country's consumers, considerably reduced tariff protection for Argentine industries. Instead, it paid special attention to stimulating agricultural and grazing production and provided particular incentives in the form of tax relief and relatively low interest loans to grazers.

General Nature of the Argentine Economy

The result of the fitful economic development of recent decades has been that Argentina's economy has not yet reached the "take-off" point, from which it could develop at a rapid pace without significant further help from abroad. In spite of the country's extensive resources and its sizable and well-educated population, Argentina today presents a picture of economic stagnation, in which economically growing sectors are offset by decaying sectors, and in which the increase in national income has at best barely kept pace with the country's slowly increasing population; in several recent years, it has even failed to do that.

The Argentine economy in the 1960's presents a mixed picture. Agriculture and grazing continue to be of key importance. Some 40 per cent of the land is devoted to pasture, and 10 per cent is under cultivation. In 1963, Argentina had some 47 million sheep, 40 million cattle, and 3 million hogs. Most of the country's exports came from the countryside. In 1964, meat made up 23 per cent of total exports; wheat, 17 per cent; corn, 12 per cent; wool, 9 per cent; vegetable oils and seeds—principally linseed and sunflower oils—9 per cent; and hides, 4 per cent.

On the pampas, most of the people live in isolated groups near the headquarters of thousands of *estancias*. Life there is relatively simple, since the people lack the main accouterments of modern living—television, movies, schools, etc.— now characteristic of the urban parts of the country. Dancing, singing, story-telling, and the *asado* (a kind of barbecue) are among the main divertissements of the people in the country.

In the easternmost portions of the pampas region, in southern Santa Fé Province, and in neighboring parts of the Province of Buenos Aires, the farms are smaller, and the population is more heavily concentrated. Social life is more intense there. The same is true of the grape-growing regions in the foothills of the Andes. In the sugar-producing Province of Tucumán, the workers live in huts on company property and their living conditions have been notoriously bad for several decades.

Most of the country's manufacturing industries are concentrated in and around the nation's principal cities. There is a particularly large concentration in greater Buenos Aires. Most of the packinghouses, as well as many textile and metallurgical factories, are located in Buenos Aires, Rosario, and La Plata. Rosario is the main center of flour milling and related industry; Córdoba has in the last two decades become the principal site of the automobile industry and of other important metal-fabricating enterprises.

Most of the country's principal manufacturing enterprises are still closely associated with agriculture or grazing. These include meat-packing, flour milling, vegetable-oil processing, and quebracho extracting. The textile industry, also based principally on Argentine-grown raw materials, cotton and wool, is the largest single manufacturing industry. Other important enterprises closely associated with Argentine agriculture include wine production, sugar refining, and various kinds of food processing. Some of these products are exported in small quantities to neighboring countries.

In recent years, Argentina has also developed other types of manufacturing. It now has a first-class steel plant at San Nicolás, which is capable of producing the raw material for many other branches of the metallurgical industry. Although Argentina must still import most of the coal and iron it uses, steel production has served as a spur both to the development of other industries using its products and to the exploration for the basic materials needed. The total Argentine output of raw steel in 1965 was 1,347,400 tons; Argentina also produced 1,237,100 tons of rolled-steel products.

Closely associated with the basic metal industries are other branches of manufacturing that make products in which Argentina is already, or is about to become, self-sufficient. These include firms for electrical and mechanical household appliances as well as automobiles. Some small ships are also built in Argentina. Automobile, machinery, and similar branches of manufacturing account for about one-sixth of

Argentina's total output and are the second largest branch of industry.

The chemical industry, based largely on the country's petroleum resources, has also become an important part of the Argentine manufacturing sector. Argentina is now virtually self-sufficient in pharmaceuticals and is also a producer of a wide variety of heavy chemicals, fertilizers, plastics, and similar products.

The type of industrialization Argentina has experienced in recent years has changed the nature of the country's manufacturing enterprises. Until at least 1930, most of the firms listed as "factories" in the economic census were, in fact, more like small workshops; only a handful of packinghouses, textile plants, flour mills, and other such enterprises were modern industrial establishments. However, due to the expansion of industry after 1930, the country now possesses, in its metallurgical and chemical industries, its cement plants, glass factories, and its greatly expanded textile industry, many relatively large modern industrial enterprises.

The economic census of 1954 showed that there were 621,329 nonagricultural firms operating in Argentina, of which 181,763 were in manufacturing and mining. These industrial firms employed 1,536,530 workers. In contrast, the 417,423 commercial enterprises had 1,230,466 employees. Although there was some industrial expansion during the Frondizi administration, the situation has not changed substantially since the 1954 census was taken. The significance of manufacturing in the total Argentine economy is shown by the fact that, in 1965, it accounted for 35.4 per cent of the total domestic product. In 1960, it employed 25.2 per cent of the total labor force.

Buenos Aires is the nation's principal commercial center as well as its capital, the focus of cultural activity, and an important manufacturing center. The country's great banks have their headquarters there. Most of the smaller cities of the interior are the commercial centers for their agricultural or grazing hinterlands, although more and more are becoming important industrial sites.

Private and Public Enterprise

In terms of ownership, Argentina has a mixed economy. Although the government owns a substantial segment of the more important enterprises, most of the country's means of production and distribution are still in the hands of private firms.

The principal reason for the incursion of the government into the economy has been the desire to protect the national interest. With the growth of popular nationalism during the first decades of the twentieth century, the conviction became widespread that such key elements of the economy as public utilities, the railroads, and heavy industry should not be left in the hands of the foreign investors who, in many cases, had originally established them.

As a result of this strong nationalist sentiment, the railroads and most of the country's public utilities were taken over by the government in the 1940's and 1950's. As we have noted, there has been a continuing struggle over whether the state should dominate the nation's petroleum industry. During the 1950's, the government undertook to establish the national steel enterprise in San Nicolás in the Province of Buenos Aires and became a partner in new automobile and agricultural-implement firms. The national airline, Aerolíneas Argentinas, the larger portion of the commercial river fleet, and important overseas shipping lines are also in public hands. But most of the economy, particularly agriculture and grazing, and wholesale and retail commerce, is still privately owned. This is also true of most of the country's manufacturing industries. Bus and truck transportation and most other services are also in private hands.

In recent years, a wide degree of skepticism has developed

concerning the extension of public ownership in the economy. This doubt largely grew because of the inefficiency, overstaffing, and deficits of the government-owned railroad system.

Labor Organization

Most of the country's manufacturing industries, as well as the railroads, airlines, and a sizable segment of agriculture and commerce, are unionized. This has been the case since the early days of the Perón era, when unionization and collective bargaining became the rule instead of the exception in the Argentine economy.

Before the Revolution of 1943, the only well-unionized parts of the economy were the railroads, some large commercial enterprises, and a scattering of industries. However, Perón built his political career by encouraging workers to organize and elaborating extensive legislation on their behalf. Since that time, workers have come to regard it as natural that they should belong to a union.

For more than two decades, the country's labor picture has been dominated by large unions, among which the organizations of metal, textile, and construction workers, of commercial employees, railwaymen, urban transport workers, and government employees have been among the most important and powerful. Most unions are members of the Confederación General del Trabajo (the General Federation of Labor), or CGT.

The unions have not only been strong in membership and political influence but also wealthy. They have been able to maintain sizable corps of paid officials and to employ lawyers, economists, engineers, and other technicians. Since the Perón period, collective bargaining has become the principal method of regulating labor-management relations. In most of the key industries, nationwide collective agreements exist. These provide the general framework for labor relations, including wages, hours, and general working conditions. They also provide for elaborate grievance procedures through which individual worker's complaints against employers are processed.

The growth of a strong labor movement has undoubtedly provided the average Argentine worker with a kind of protection against arbitrary actions by his employer which he did not possess before. Unions have given the worker recourse against dismissal, discrimination, and other kinds of grievances, which every worker encounters from time to time. At certain periods, the unions have also been able to provide the workers with improvements in their working and living conditions, which they could not have achieved as individuals.

However, the labor movement has also played other roles of major significance. Elsewhere in this study, we will pay special attention to the political activities of the unions since the beginning of the Perón era. Here, it is sufficient to note the participation of the unions in the adaptation of the worker to an entirely new environment.

Most of the workers who have entered Argentine industries during the last three decades have been migrants from the countryside. There, they were accustomed to a paternalistic relationship with their employers, to whom they could turn for help in any crisis. When a worker came to the city to work in a factory, or on the railroad, or in a store, he encountered a new kind of impersonal relationship with his employer which was strange and sometimes frightening to him. Furthermore, the living conditions in large cities were very different from those he had been accustomed to.

The unions gave the new industrial workers some place to turn. Not only did they offer protection against abuse, but they also frequently offered medical help, legal aid, and family counseling services. They helped the workers to become accustomed to the unfamiliar discipline of factory life; they often provided vacation resorts where they could spend paid vacations, which the unions and Juan Perón had won for them. In general, it may be said that the unions played an important role in converting country bumpkins into urban industrial workers.

Deterioration of the Infrastructure

In spite of the considerable progress Argentina has made in manufacturing, key sectors of the economy, such as the national railway system, have undergone almost steady deterioration during the last twenty-five years. Although Argentina still has the largest railway system in Latin America and the seventh largest in the world—some 28,068 miles of road— it is in a notoriously run-down condition. The British and French firms that once controlled more than two-thirds of the Argentine railroads had allowed them to deteriorate during the last quarter of a century of their ownership. Thus, by 1940, several years before the rail lines were nationalized, two-thirds of the railway engines were over fourteen years old, and half that number dated from the very first years of this century. Almost no new engines were purchased during the following fifteen years. What was true of the rolling stock was likewise true of the rails and other fixed railroad equipment.

Since the 1940's, succeeding governments have made sporadic efforts to rehabilitate and re-equip the railways. However, the country's political instability has prevented any government from following through with any consistency a program for the reorganization and reconstruction of the national rail network. In 1955, it was estimated that it would cost $1.5 billion to put the railroads back into adequate condition. Nothing approaching that sum has, however, been spent for this purpose in the meanwhile.

The result of this situation is disastrous. Breakdowns of service are frequent; schedules that are now about 50 per cent slower than they were thirty years ago are not kept; rolling stock and other equipment are old and in some cases decrepit—in April, 1964, it was estimated that 20 per cent of the freight cars and 36.5 per cent of the diesel engines were out of action, awaiting repair. Accidents are all too frequent. By 1964, the railroads were carrying only a little more than half the freight traffic of ten years before.

In addition, the nationalized railways have for two decades contributed heavily to the government's sizable annual budget deficit. In 1964, the operating deficit of the railroads, which must be borne by the government treasury, amounted to some 75 million pesos.

The situation with regard to the railways is largely duplicated in the highway system. Although sizable programs of road building were carried out in the 1930's, which gave Argentina then one of the most extensive highway systems in Latin America, little has been done to improve the road network since that time. Indeed, the condition of the highways has declined drastically. By 1945, although the country had 38,000 miles of road, less than one-seventh had any paving. Subsequently, many of those roads that had been in good condition at the end of World War II were allowed to deteriorate, so that by the 1960's, the highway system was considerably worse than it had been twenty years before.

For a long time the state of motor vehicles operating in Argentina was also poor. In 1945, about 50 per cent of trucks had been in use for fifteen years; sporadic imports in subsequent years did not do much to improve this situation. Between the 1930's and the 1950's, the number of cars per capita in Argentina declined by about one-third.

In recent years, there has been some improvement in the automobile situation. With the establishment of the Kaiser plant in Córdoba, in the mid-1950's, and subsequently of other automobile firms, during the Frondizi period, the number of cars in use has increased substantially. However, the immensity of the problem can be seen from the fact that the national automobile industry now turns out about 11,000 cars per month, while virtually no cars are imported—but the total number of passenger cars in service in 1963 was 697,700, and the number of trucks was 512,300. At current rates of production, it would take almost ten years to replace all of the vehicles now in operation.

The river fleet, another key means of transportation of particular importance to Argentina, has also been neglected. Although in the early years of the Perón administration many modern ships were added to this fleet, very little has been done since that time. In the mid-1960's, the river fleet consisted of some 216 vessels, with a total weight of more than 1.2 million tons.

The city streets of Buenos Aires and other major cities are also in bad repair. Potholes, endless repair projects, and interrupted traffic are all too characteristic of the conditions of the streets in most of the country's major cities.

Argentine public utilities have declined in an equally disastrous manner. The telephones are particularly notorious for their malfunctioning. It has become commonplace for large sections of Buenos Aires to be without telephone service for weeks and sometimes months. The waiting list for new telephones is years' long.

The deterioration of the infrastructure is not the only indication of the crisis through which the Argentine economy is passing. The virtual cessation of the growth of the national income and the country's nagging inflation are other indices.

The Inflation Problem

Inflation has been a problem of major importance since the late 1940's. During the early years of the Perón administration, the government kept such tendencies in check by subsidizing major food products and important nationally produced raw materials. At that time, too, the ample foreign-exchange resources made it possible to import large quantities of goods, which also served to keep price increases under control.

However, by 1949, Argentina's foreign-exchange reserves had been largely exhausted, and the decline in agricultural and meat production made it increasingly difficult for Argentina to meet its commitments abroad and at the same time to provide the growing quantities needed by its own population. As a result of these factors, prices began to rise rapidly. The upshot of the inflation during the latter years of the Perón administration was a fall in the real wages of Argentine workers. Although real wages had increased between 1943 and 1949, by the time Perón was overthrown, in 1955, they had fallen back to approximately the level prevailing before the Perón era. For skilled workers, the real wage tended to be even less than that of 1943. This situation continued to deteriorate after the fall of Perón.

The Perón government was the first that tried to come to grips with this problem. Its initial move was an attempt to curb wage increases and to break any strikes aimed at obtaining wage boosts which the government had not sanctioned. By 1952, the government had gone even farther. It rationed meat and grain consumed in the country by instituting meatless days and by severely restricting the amount of grain available to millers for domestic consumption. At the same time, Perón fixed the prices of a wide range of goods and carried on a somewhat sporadic campaign against merchants who did not adhere to the price ceilings. Finally, the Perón regime also sought to obtain help from abroad, both from private investors and international lending agencies.

However, these measures largely failed. There is little question that the inflation of the early 1950's did much to discredit the Perón regime among its labor followers, and it helps to explain why these followers did not rally to the defense of the regime when it was menaced with the military insurrection of September, 1955, that finally overthrew Perón.

The provisional governments from 1955 to 1958 tried to resolve the inflationary situation by re-establishing the policy of economic liberalism. Particular stress was laid on encouraging greater production and productivity in the countryside. Prices offered to grazers and grain growers were drastically increased, and steps were taken to re-establish a free market for agricultural produce. However, the inflation continued to mount during these three years.

Frondizi's Anti-inflation Program

The first six months of the Frondizi regime, which came to power on May 1, 1958, were marked by an intensified spurt of inflation. This was due, in part at least, to the fact that Frondizi was forced in some measure to fulfill his election promises of granting a 60 per cent wage increase to all Argentine workers. Although the increases actually given fell considerably short of this mark, they were nonetheless substantial enough to provide a considerable impetus to existing inflationary tendencies.

Late in 1958, President Frondizi had become convinced that drastic measures had to be taken if the galloping level of prices was to be curbed. He also felt that any such program had to include two aspects: price stabilization and economic rehabilitation and development. During the succeeding three years, the government pursued these two objectives simultaneously.

The Frondizi price-stabilization program was a stringent one. On the one hand, it involved the attempt to freeze wages after an initial cost-of-living increase had been granted. On the other hand, it involved a sharp restriction on credit. This was exercised in such a way as to make funds readily available to selected enterprises which, in the opinion of the government, would be particularly significant for economic development, but would limit the over-all volume of credit.

A third aspect of the Frondizi stabilization program involved the attempt to bring the government budget more nearly into balance. To do so, it was particularly important to reduce the deficits in the government-owned economic enterprises, such as the railroads, and the Frondizi government therefore sold some of the enterprises under its control. It also worked out a program for the reorganization and rationalization of the nation's railroad system.

There is no question that the price-stabilization and economic-development programs of the Frondizi government were interrelated. The relaxation of pressure on the balance of payments through oil-development programs and the enticement of considerable foreign investment in manufacturing and public utilities certainly contributed to internal price stabilization. Similarly, indications that price rises were being halted engendered confidence among both foreign and domestic entrepreneurs in the viability of possible new investment and so stimulated economic development.

The Frondizi program was successful in reducing the rate of inflation. During 1961, prices rose only about 13 per cent compared with 27 per cent in 1957 and more than 100 per cent from 1958 to 1959. After March, 1962, when President Frondizi was overthrown, the rhythm of inflation once again quickened.

A continuing price rise plagued the governments of Presidents José María Guido (1962–63) and Arturo Illia (1963–66). Although Illia's administration did not undertake the drastic kind of program attempted by Frondizi, even mild attempts to limit wage increases and credit expansion met strong resistance from the unions and from some businessmen. There is no doubt that Illia's unwillingness to take decisive economic measures contributed considerably to his overthrow by the armed forces in June, 1966.

After about six months of hesitation, early in 1967, the military government of General Juan Carlos Onganía announced its intention to undertake one more price-stabilization program. It involved the usual formulas of wage freezing, limitations on credit, and attempts to restrict government expenditures. It ran into strong opposition from organized labor, but in a showdown, in February, 1967, the government succeeded in breaking the unions' resistance. By the end of 1967, the Onganía government's stabilization program began to slow down price increases but had also provoked considerable unemployment.

The inability to keep prices in check remains one of Argentina's principal problems. It is more pressing than might otherwise be the case, because, unlike the situation in Brazil during the 1940's and 1950's, Argentina's inflation has not been accompanied by rapid economic development. Rather, Argentina has gotten the worst of both worlds, so to speak, having large-scale price increases and a relatively stagnant economy.

Devaluation

A corollary of the constantly rising price level within Argentina has been the equally constant decline of the international value of the Argentine peso. To a considerable degree, the former has been the cause of the latter. Because of the increase in the prices of goods in Argentina, the country has been in constant danger that these high prices may so raise the cost of Argentine exports as to make them uncompetitive in international markets. It has therefore been frequently necessary to lower the value of the peso itself, thus enabling the pound, dollar, or franc to purchase more pesos and acting as a partial offset to the increase in Argentine domestic prices.

An even more important cause of devaluation has been Argentina's balance of payments, chronically awry since the late 1940's. Decreasing exports and the fact that there has been no comparable decline of imports have meant that there has been a constant desire for Argentina to buy more than it sells. This tendency has been partly offset by international loans and foreign investments, but these have come only in a sporadic fashion. They have certainly not been sufficient to prevent a more or less steady decline in the exchange value of the peso.

This decline has been drastic. In the mid-1940's, the exchange rate was five pesos to the dollar. By the end of the Perón regime one dollar could purchase more than ten times as many pesos. After 1955, the peso fell still further, although the Frondizi administration was able to stabilize its international value at eighty pesos to the dollar. After Frondizi's overthrow, Argentine currency tumbled again, and by mid-1967, the New York rate of exchange for the peso was close to 350 pesos to the dollar.

The Trends of National Income

The crisis of the Argentine economy is also underlined by the fitful behavior of the country's gross national product, and, particularly, by the per-capita income of the average Argentine. For nearly two decades, the rise in the total annual output of goods and services has been smaller than the increase each year in the country's population, although the growth of Argentina's population is one of the slowest in Latin America.

According to figures developed by the Chase Manhattan Bank, the annual increase in Argentina's gross domestic product during the decade 1950–60 amounted to two-tenths of 1 per cent. If one compares this almost negligible rise with the population increase of 2.34 per cent per year, the developments during this decade become all too clear. The annual amount of goods and services available to the average Argentine dropped considerably. Between 1960 and 1966, the per-capita income increase was still only about 1 per cent a year. Although, in 1965, the growth of the economy reached 7 per cent, this was more a reflection of good crops than of any basic improvement. The political disturbances in 1966 certainly made it difficult to maintain as substantial an increase in the national output as before.

It is probably true that most Argentines have not yet felt as directly as one might have expected the effect of this stagnation in the growth of the national economy. The decline is reflected in the continued reduction of the country's capital—in its railroads, roads, telephones, and perhaps in the failure to replace machinery and other equipment in older industries—more than in the actual availability of goods and services to the average Argentine. He still eats well, is decently clothed, and, for the most part, lives in a reasonably good dwelling.

Yet even this is beginning to change. There is little doubt that the housing crisis has grown increasingly bad. Except very sporadically, little new housing has been constructed since the giant low-cost housing efforts early in the Perón administration. Certainly, the average city dweller suffers from the inefficient operations of the electricity and telephone systems in many of the country's cities, and it becomes increasingly difficult for him to take advantage of the vacation opportunities to which he has been legally entitled since the Perón period.

If the stagnation of the country's economy continues for very much longer, the average Argentine will suffer from it more and more. As the population continues to grow and the sum total of goods and services lags behind, the struggle over the division of the national output will become more intense and bitter. The costs of things that the average Argentine buys will continue to climb while his wage or salary will falter, and the inefficiency of the public services will become more and more of a burden.

Conclusion

The key to Argentina's continuing economic stagnation is political. On the one hand, economic development through industrialization and the building of a thoroughly diversified economy has not become a national credo as in some other Latin American countries; and on the other, powerful political elements associated with grazing and agriculture still seriously question the appropriateness of this kind of a policy.

Yet more important is the fact that the constant meddling of the military in politics—a situation that has been intensified since 1955 by the widespread fear of a possible return of Perón—has not allowed the government to follow a consistent development policy long enough to make it successful. It seems likely that so long as the fear of Perón's return continues to haunt national politics, and so long as the military are called upon with increasing frequency to overturn the established government, it will be impossible to create the kind of leadership that can complete the work of economic development and social change.

IV

Politics and Government

The first thing to note about the politics and government in Argentina is the contrast between theory and practice. The second major fact is that the governmental structure and political life of the country have been in a state of crisis since 1930.

The Formal Structure of Government

According to its constitution, Argentina is a federal democratic republic. Although the model for this constitution, which, except for one short interval, has been in effect since 1853, is that of the U.S. constitution, it functions very differently from its prototype.* According to the Argentine constitution, the president of the republic is elected every six years, and he cannot be re-elected until at least one intervening term has ensued. He is chosen, together with a vice-president, by an electoral college, as in the United States. The president, who must be a native-born Argentine, is the chief executive officer of the republic. He names and dismisses members of the cabinet, who, according to the constitution, are eight in number. In fact, however, the cabinet is augmented by a number of secretaries, who are in theory on a lower hierarchical level than the ministers but are in fact

---

* It should be noted that the military dictatorship of General Juan Carlos Onganía, which took power in June, 1966, with the avowed intention of staying in office for ten years, issued a "revolutionary statute" which, for the time being, largely supersedes the constitution.

equal in status. According to the constitution, the president
is also the commander-in-chief of the armed forces.

Congress consists of two houses, the Chamber of Deputies
and the Senate. The former is chosen on the basis of the population of the various provinces; each province has two members in the Senate. Except in the federal capital, the city of
Buenos Aires, where senators are elected by popular vote, the
constitution provides that senators are to be chosen by the
provincial legislators; this provision is similar to that existing
in the United States before 1913.

The judicial system is headed by a Supreme Court, and
subsidiary courts are established by Congress. The members
of the Supreme Court are appointed by the president and
confirmed by the Senate and enjoy life tenure. In theory, the
three powers of government are equal and independent.
However, as we shall see, there has been a consistent tendency in Argentina for the executive branch to predominate.

The constitution proclaims that Argentina has a federal
form of government. There are twenty-three provinces and a
federal district, the city of Buenos Aires. Each province has
its own constitution, and each province elects its own legisla-
ture and governor. The provinces have considerable power
in the fields of public works, health, education, and in the
use and development of their natural resources. For some
decades, however, the tendency has been to reduce the constitutional powers of the provinces. Under Perón, the provinces lost control over labor relations, and under Frondizi,
they were deprived of the right to regulate the use and determine the ownership of petroleum resources within their
borders.

The constitution contains a bill of rights, providing for
freedom of speech, press, and assembly. Although Argentina
is a Catholic country, and the president and vice-president
must be Roman Catholics, believers in all other religions, as
well as atheists, are free to follow their own consciences, pub-

licly and privately. The Argentine constitution, however, also contains a provision permitting the government to suspend the rights of individuals under certain circumstances. This can be done either on a local scale or throughout the nation.

For almost fifty years, the electoral system on the Argentine law books was unique. It provided that the party that received the largest number of votes in each province, was also entitled to send two-thirds of the province's delegates to the Chamber of Deputies; the second largest party was given the remaining one-third. However, in the election for a constituent assembly in 1957, and in the general election of 1963, the system of proportional representation was instituted. As a result of this, more than twenty parties were represented in the Chamber, whereas before that no more than six parties had such representation.

Elections are conducted on the basis of universal adult suffrage. Before Perón came to power, women were not allowed to vote. During the early years of her husband's regime, Evita Perón waged a strenuous campaign for woman suffrage, which was granted in the Peronista constitution of 1949. When the 1853 constitution was reinstituted after Perón's overthrow, the document was changed to incorporate voting rights for women.

The Realities of Government Since 1930

The realities of Argentine government and politics are markedly different from the formal structure provided in the constitution of 1853. This has been particularly true since 1930. In the nearly four decades since then, which constitutionally should have encompassed all or parts of seven successive administrations, there have, in fact, been fifteen different presidents. Of these fifteen, only one, General Agustín P. Justo (1932–38), was elected and gave his office to an elected successor. Another, General Juan Perón

(1946–55) was elected and filled out his first term but was overthrown before he could finish his second term. Six of the fifteen presidents between 1930 and 1967 came to power by virtue of *coups d'état;* these were José F. Uriburu (1930–32), General Arturo Rawson (1943), General Pedro Ramírez (1943–44), General Eduardo Lonardi (1955), José María Guido (1962–63), and General Juan Carlos Onganía (1966–   ). Eight presidents during this period were overthrown by coups. Hipólito Irigoyen (1928–30), Ramón S. Castillo (1941–43), General Arturo Rawson, General Pedro Ramírez, General Juan Perón, General Eduardo Lonardi, Arturo Frondizi (1958–62), and Arturo Illia (1963–66).

Even those presidents elected to office did not come to power as the result of normal elections. The Radical Party (UCR), which was then the country's major party, was not allowed to participate in the 1932 election; it is generally agreed that the 1938 election was won by fraud; the 1951 election was held in an atmosphere of terror which raised grave doubts about its validity; and the Peronista Party, then the largest in the country, was not allowed candidates in the 1958 and 1963 elections. Only the 1946 election, in which Juan Perón first won the presidency, was honest and relatively free from coercion, but even in that case, the campaign leading up to it had been marked by considerable violence and terror on both sides.

Since 1930, the legislative branch of the Argentine Government has had no more "normal" an existence than the executive. Congress was dissolved in 1930 by a government that had seized power by a coup, and it did not function at all for two years. Congress was again dissolved after the coup of 1943 and did not meet until 1946. The same situation occurred after the overthrow of Perón in 1955, and it was only in 1958 that another Congress was elected. Congress was again dissolved by President Guido in 1962, and a year passed before another Congress sat. In 1966, General Juan

Carlos Onganía dissolved Congress upon seizing power and even dissolved the supreme electoral board since he did not intend to hold any further elections—no such body was therefore needed.

Even when Congress existed, its representativeness was open to question. The majority party, the UCR, was not represented between 1932–38 because it had not been allowed to participate in the 1932 poll. The two opposition senators elected in 1946 were not allowed by the Peronista majority to take their seats; and subsequent congressional elections during the Perón period were so rigged as to be of doubtful validity. The Peronistas were not allowed to take part in constituent assembly and congressional elections in 1957 and 1958; when they made a very strong showing in the 1962 elections, the results of the election were canceled.

The courts have fared only a little better than the executive and legislative branches of the government. Twice since 1930 the Supreme Court was ousted, once by impeachment under Perón, in 1946, and the second time by decree of General Onganía, in 1966. On various occasions, judges of lower courts were removed or disciplined for making decisions unpalatable to the regime in power.

The courts have been faced with a particularly difficult situation as a result of *de facto* governments during recent decades. Obviously, such governments exist in violation of the constitution. After each coup, the courts, and particularly the Supreme Court, have therefore been faced with the question of the constitutional validity of the acts and decrees of these regimes. Usually, they have found a basis for judging them legitimate.

The principle of federalism has also suffered because of the instability of Argentine governments since 1930. Each coup has been an occasion to replace provincial governors by nominees of the new regime, whether or not the ousted provincial executives had been elected or appointed by a previous *de facto* regime. The provincial legislatures have had the same interrupted pattern of operation as the national Congress, and the provincial courts, like the federal courts, have not been immune to the purges and other abuses.

The governmental and political crisis in Argentina has many causes, of which three are probably the most important. The first concerns the difficulty the country has encountered in making the transition from a predominantly agricultural exporting nation to a mixed agricultural and industrial economy, and the shifts in class alignment and power that this transformation involves. The second problem has been the division brought about by Perón in public opinion between his enthusiastic supporters and his violent opponents, and the fears this split engendered on both sides. And, finally, there has been the fact that these two problems have helped to provoke endemic militarism.

Struggle over Industrialization and Social Reform

Even before World War I manufacturing had begun to undermine the pre-eminence of the Argentine rural exporting community. World War I intensified economic growth outside the areas of grazing and agriculture, and with the onslaught of the Great Depression, manufacturing grew apace, and with it, the economic and political influence of the industrialists and the urban working class.

During most of the 1860–1930 period, power was firmly in the hands of the large landholding class. Although in 1916 the landowners' Conservative Party lost control of the presidency, UCR President Hipólito Irigoyen did not have the majority in Congress which would have permitted him to enact any fundamental changes. The second UCR administration of President Marcelo T. de Alvear was also not anxious to upset the traditional balance of power. In 1930, after the overthrow of President Irigoyen, who had returned to office in 1928, the government once again came under the influence of rural interests.

During the 1930's, landlord interests and the Conservatives controlled economic and social policy, and the conflict between the landowners and the middle and working classes became increasingly clear. The manufacturing interests wanted government protection, as well as facilities for obtaining necessary credit. They also needed rapid expansion of the economic infrastructure, especially of the production of electricity, gas, and other fuels. The growing working class also impatiently demanded legislation on its behalf. It wanted protective laws, as well as social security. There was likewise an increasing need for a government ministry to deal with labor-management problems.

The Conservative governments were not responsive to the desires of the middle and working classes. Quite to the contrary, these administrations followed policies that were frankly opposed to the interests of the manufacturers and largely ignored the welfare of the workers. The governments of the 1930's refused to implement the pressing demands for a protective tariff policy, believing that Argentina was destined to remain a grazing and agricultural country, which should continue to import manufactured goods from Europe, particularly from Great Britain. The fear was expressed that any moves to protect industrial goods produced in Argentina would provoke British retaliation in the form of Britain's refusal to buy Argentine agricultural exports.

The governments of the 1930's also turned a deaf ear to growing demands for labor and social legislation. With the support of the Socialists and of some Radicals in Congress, union leaders repeatedly proposed the establishment of an adequate social security system. Socialist legislators and some newspapermen pointed again and again to the deplorable working conditions existing in certain parts of the republic—particularly among Tucumán sugar workers, quebracho workers in the Chaco, and yerba mate pickers in the Mesopotamia area—and demanded government action to protect them. Labor leaders also sought a sympathetic attitude from the government for the right of collective bargaining. However, the governments of the time ignored all these matters with the result that, by the early 1940's, Argentina was the most backward of the larger Latin American countries insofar as labor and social legislation was concerned.

The Conservative Party

During the half-century or more before Perón's military coup of June 4, 1943, the growing conflict between the landed and the growing middle and working classes was reflected in the political parties. The party of the rural landlords was the Conservative Party, which controlled the national government completely until 1916.

However, the Conservative Party was not merely the party of the rural interests. Domingo Faustino Sarmiento and others of the group that came to power in 1862 and from whom the Conservative Party was directly descended had given another characteristic to the organization: They wanted to "Europeanize" Argentina. Sarmiento and others of his generation were strongly opposed to what they considered the "savagery" of the traditional gaucho, who had been dominant during the regime of Juan Manuel Rosas. They felt that the solution to the problems of the country was to populate Argentina with Europeans, who would reduce the previously dominant role of the mestizos. They also sought to create a literate, European-oriented population.

There was no conflict between the Conservatives' role as spokesman for the landed interests and their attempts to Europeanize Argentina. The landlords needed large numbers of immigrants to work their grain fields and cattle ranches. The exporting interests of the landowners tied them closely to Europe, particularly to Great Britain.

The Radicals

The Unión Cívica Radical (UCR), or Radical Party, which until the *coup d'état* of June 4, 1943, constituted the principal opposition to the Conservatives, differed from them both in social origins and in its views on the cultural orientation of Argentina. The UCR drew much of its support and most of its leadership from the middle class. In the small towns and cities of the interior, the school teacher, the merchant, and frequently some of the lawyers belonged to the UCR. So did many of the artisans, from whom emerged the new industrial class, as well as a sizable segment of the working class.

The Radicals also represented Argentine nationalism against the European orientation of the Conservatives. Although drawing considerable support from immigrant workers in the cities, they did not share the Conservative belief in the necessity for converting Argentina into a South American version of a European nation. Hipólito Irigoyen, for nearly forty years the leader of the party, particularly represented this "American" orientation of the party.

The Socialists

The Socialist Party, the only other party of some significance between the 1890's and the coup of 1943, differed from both the Conservatives and the Radicals. The Socialist Party was at least formally Marxist in its ideology, and its founder, Juan B. Justo, was the first translator of *Das Kapital* into Spanish. In conformity with its ideology, the Socialists were very active in the labor movement. In 1890, the Socialists had established the country's first national labor confederation, the Federación Obrera de la República Argentina (FORA), before the Socialist Party had even been formally established. However, in 1901, FORA was captured by anarchosyndicalists, who changed its name to Federación Obrera Regional Argentina. The Socialists thereupon organized their own group, the Unión General de Trabajadores (UGT).

After 1909, the Socialist influence in the labor movement declined for more than a decade, but the party's electoral influence increased. In 1904, the party had elected its first member to the Chamber of Deputies, and eight years later, it elected its first senator and several more deputies.

After 1922, the Socialists dominated the labor movement, maintaining their control until the rise of Perón. Throughout the whole period 1894–1943, the Socialists were the principal political spokesmen of the urban working class, particularly of Buenos Aires.

Although aligned with the Radicals in opposition to the dominating landlord-controlled Conservative Party, the Socialists shared the Conservative belief in the need for Europeanizing Argentina. This was probably due to the large numbers of immigrants who flocked to the Socialists' ranks and to the Socialists' universalist philosophy, which made them deprecate patriotism and nationalism in all its forms.

The European orientation and internationalist philosophy of the Socialists contributed considerably to their decline after 1943. Although these attitudes and ideas were appropriate for a working-class party, representing largely immigrants from Italy and Spain, they were no longer attractive to the labor groups in Argentina in the early 1940's. By then, the workers were no longer mostly immigrants but children of immigrants or migrants from the interior of Argentina, without previous experiences with trade unions or radical ideas. Both groups tended to be nationalist in their outlook and to reject the Europeanizing tendencies and the internationalist ideas of the Socialists. This became very apparent once Juan Domingo Perón arrived on the political scene.

The Economic and Social Policies of Perón

The *coup d'état* of June 4, 1943 fundamentally changed the political alignments that had existed before. Although the coup was provoked by factors that had nothing to do with the economic and social issues dividing public opinion in the 1930's, it resulted in a fundamental shift in political power. It also resulted in the meteoric rise to political prominence of Juan Domingo Perón and in the splitting of all classes and pre-1943 political groups into pro- and anti-Peronista factions. Finally, the turbulence that came in the wake of the 1943 coup intensified the growing trend toward military domination of Argentine political life.

The regime established in June, 1943, in which Colonel Juan Perón soon became the dominant figure, and which catapulted him into the presidency in June, 1946, followed economic and social policies diametrically opposed to those of the Conservative regimes of the 1930's. On the one hand, the Perón regime gave strong encouragement to industrialization. It raised protective tariffs and used part of the profits of its export monopoly, IAPI, to provide foreign exchange for industrialists who wished to import machinery and other capital equipment. It developed the country's natural gas resources and built a pipeline to bring the gas to the industries in and near Buenos Aires. It established the Banco Industrial, which made liberal loans to manufacturing enterprises throughout the country.

In the social field, the Perón regime strongly encouraged the growth of the trade-union movement and, during its early years, forced employers to sign agreements advantageous to the workers. It also enacted a broad body of labor legislation and established an extensive social security system.

As a result of its economic policies, the Perón regime won substantial support among the industrialists. Because of the extensive aid to industrialization, many industrialists overcame their hesitation with regard to Perón's pro-labor activities. Thus, many of the manufacturers who had traditionally supported the UCR swung around to at least passive support for the Perón administration, while a minority openly collaborated with the regime.

The social aspects of the Perón program won the support of most workers, and it was therefore possible for Perón to win control over the largest central labor organization, the Confederación General del Trabajo (CGT) and over most of its constituent organizations within less than a year of the June 4, 1943 coup. His support for the expansion of the trade-union movement, his enactment, by decree, of much social and labor legislation, and his emphasis on Argentine nationalism contributed to the growth of his influence among the workers.

However, most of the middle class was not won over to Perón. The principal reason for this would seem to be the dictatorial nature of his regime. Quite unnecessarily, Perón, who could have ruled as a democrat, became more and more oppressive as his administration continued. He destroyed freedom of press and assembly and turned the legislatures and courts into mere tools of his administration. He instituted a reign of terror against the critics of his administration, a situation under which the middle class suffered most. It was the dictatorial nature of the regime that drove many of the potential sympathizers of his social and economic program into unalterable opposition.

This polarization of public opinion as a result of the dictatorial nature of Perón's regime was most unfortunate for Argentina. It split those elements in the Argentine body politic which might otherwise have united in support of economic development and social reform, and it raised an issue in Argentine public life after 1955—whether or not Perón would be allowed to return to power—that cut across all other alignments.

Perón's Political Impact

The rise of Perón and his support from the working class deprived the Socialist Party of its traditional backing. Although some workers remained with the Socialists, the party became a fundamentally middle-class organization. Similarly, the Radicals lost some of their backing from industrialists, as well as from the working class. The impact of Peronismo was probably most felt by the Conservatives, however. The *coup d'état* of June 4, 1943 deposed the regime in which they had shared control with military leaders for thirteen years. It deprived them of the power to "fix" elections in the provinces, and the spread of Perón's popularity among rural workers made it impossible for the landlords to get their workers to vote for the Conservative candidates favored by the landowners. As a result, the Conservative Party (known after 1930 as the National Democratic Party) was reduced to the status of a minor party. After the overthrow of Perón, the Conservatives did not emerge as a single national party, but as a loose group of provincial parties known as the Federation of Parties of the Center.

As a result of the dictatorial nature of the Perón regime, all opposition parties—Conservatives, Radicals, Socialists, and Progressive Democrats—conspired jointly and separately to overthrow the regime. They joined forces with military men who were against the Perón government, thus undermining the anti-militarist predispositions of many of the country's leading politicians. Most of the opposition groups also tended to oppose virtually everything that Perón did. Thus, few of the opposition political leaders, not even the Socialists, were willing to concede that Perón had done anything effective on behalf of the organized workers. Nor did they find any virtue in his economic measures, including those designed to step up industrialization.

Splits in the Anti-Peronista Parties

However, there were elements in all anti-Peronista parties who realized that Perón had won over an appreciable portion of the Argentine body politic, and that he had done so by stressing social issues and nationalism, particularly in the economic field. They felt therefore that it was necessary to make overtures to the Peronistas—although not necessarily to Perón himself—to admit the social advances and some economic progress, while opposing his dictatorial ambitions, and behavior. To use a different phrase, these elements felt that it was necessary to prove to the Peronista workers that Perón was not their only political friend. After the overthrow of Perón, in September, 1955, bitter controversies arose in the Radical, Socialist, Conservative, and Christian Democratic ranks between this group and the other groups that were uncompromisingly opposed not only to Perón but also to the Peronistas.

Splits occurred within all anti-Peronista parties. The UCR broke up into the at first uncompromisingly anti-Peronista UCR del Pueblo and the more amenable UCR Intransigente. The Socialists split into the Partido Socialista Argentino (PSA), which made overtures to the Peronistas, and the Partido Socialista Democrático (PSD), which opposed this line of action. The PSA subsequently split several times more. The Conservatives broke into the Federation of Center Parties and the Popular Conservative Movement, the former adamantly anti-Peronista, the latter seeking to curry Peronista favor. The Christian Democrats also split, the majority seeking Peronista support and the minority withdrawing from all political activity.

The original split in these parties, provoked largely by the question of how to deal with the Peronistas, did not necessarily determine their continuing position. Thus, in the election of 1963, the UCR del Pueblo sought avidly to win Peronista support, and President Illia continued to court the Peronistas after winning that election. Both factions of the Conservatives were also actively seeking to win over Peronistas by the early 1960's. Even the PSD, headed by Americo Ghioldi, and probably the most adamantly anti-Peronista party in Argentine politics, was by 1966 making distinctions between "good" Peronistas and "bad" Peronistas.

The one thing upon which virtually all non-Peronista parties agreed was that under no circumstances could Juan Perón be allowed to come back to power. In practice, this meant that so long as Perón remained alive, even though in exile, the Peronistas would not be allowed to win the presidency or control the Congress. This firm resolution put even those non-Peronista leaders who were most prone to seek Peronista support in a somewhat equivocal position, since it limited the extent to which they could ever cooperate with the Peronistas so long as Perón lived. It also made political leaders who theoretically believed in democracy willing to see quite undemocratic means used to keep the Peronistas out of power.

The Peronistas

However, this implacable determination of non-Peronistas not to allow the return of Perón also had its impact on the Peronistas. It certainly contributed to a major split among them, which occurred late in 1965 and early in 1966, the first such division in their ranks to take place since the party had been organized twenty years before.

The Peronista Party was organized in 1946 by the merger of the three groups that had supported Perón in his presidential campaign earlier in 1946. These were the Partido Laborista (Labor Party), the Unión Cívica Radical Renovada, and the Partido Independiente (Independent Party). This unification was ordered by Perón himself; it was resisted

only by a small group of trade unionists, who were led by
Cipriano Reyes, vice-president of the Labor Party and leader
of the packing-house workers. However, this resistance did
not gain much support from the rank and file Peronistas.

When Perón was in office, the Peronista Party was not a
major power factor in the regime. Much more significant
were the organized labor movement and the armed forces.
The Partido Peronista (Peronista Party) and the Partido
Peronista Feminino (Women's Peronista Party), organized by
the President's wife, Evita, to rally support among the country's women, were mainly valuable for work at election time
and as a framework within which to organize members of
Congress, of state legislatures, and of municipal councils.

The Peronista Party was not an elite group, such as the
Communist Party is in Marxist-Leninist totalitarian regimes.
Any supporter of the Peronista regime, or for that matter
anyone who wanted to appear sympathetic to the regime,
could join the two Peronista parties. These parties never
served as an instrument to "institutionalize" the Perón revolution in the way Communist and Fascist parties have done
in other countries.

With the overthrow of Perón, the two Peronista parties
were outlawed. However, an underground movement continued. There developed also a number of parties led by ex-
Peronistas who had broken with Perón at some point during
his administration, and who, after September, 1955, sought
to win influence among the Peronista workers. The two
most important of these were the Labor Party, revived by
Cipriano Reyes, and the Unión Popular (Popular Union)
founded by Juan Bramuglia, who had been a labor lawyer
before Perón and was foreign minister during the early years
of Perón's presidency. Although the Labor Party made little
headway, the Popular Union became an important vehicle
for some Peronistas after Bramuglia's death.

The underground central command of the Peronistas remained in close contact with Perón, and at various moments of crisis they followed his orders closely. They passed along orders not only to boycott the 1957 constitutional assembly election but also to vote for Frondizi in February, 1958, to support so-called neo-Peronista candidates in the March, 1962, elections, which brought about the overthrow of Frondizi, and to work together with Frondizi, the Popular Conservatives, and other elements in the 1963 election.

However, by late 1965, some of the Peronista trade-union leaders became convinced that it was necessary for the future of the Peronista movement and for a national Peronista Party to achieve legal recognition and to be able to participate in the normal give and take of the country's political life. The leader of this group was Augusto Vandor, the head of the Metallurgical Workers Union, who argued that the Peronista movement would go on long after its founder's death, and that a party should therefore be established before Perón died, so that chaos would not overtake the movement upon his death. Furthermore, Vandor maintained that it was necessary to have a local leadership in Argentina even before Perón's disappearance that would be responsible for solving all but the most serious problems later confronting the movement. He also argued that a legal party leadership could perform this function.

Vandor launched this suggestion late in 1965, and in the beginning it seemed to have the general support of the Peronista ranks; the exiled dictator even gave his tentative approval. However, Perón soon abandoned the idea, apparently fearing the development of a leadership in Argentina that would not be completely subject to his control. As a result, a rival group, known as the Peronistas A los Pies de Perón (Peronistas at the Feet of Perón), was established under the leadership of José Alonso, secretary-general of the CGT, from which post he was subsequently ousted by the pro-Vandor forces.

The most dramatic conflict between these two Peronista

factions came in the provincial elections of March, 1966. The Vandor forces named a full list of candidates in the Province of Mendoza, which was expected to win control of the province. Shortly before the election, however, the Alonso group entered a rival list of nominees. The provincial government, hoping that the split would weaken the Peronistas, allowed the broadcasting of recorded speeches by Perón favoring the Alonso faction. As a result, the Alonso group ran ahead of the better organized Vandor candidates, although both groups lost to the Federation of Parties of the Center, the traditionally strong conservative party in the province.

After the seizure of power by Onganía in June, 1966, both Peronista factions tentatively backed the new military regime. Subsequently the Vandor-Alonso division among the Peronistas virtually disappeared. They united in opposition to the Onganía government but in opposition also to an all-out confrontation between organized labor and the *de facto* regime.

Early in 1968 the CGT split, largely over the question of whether the labor movement should declare all-out war on the Onganía government. The Alonso and Vandor Peronistas joined with ex-Socialists, ex-syndicalists, and other traditional anti-Peronistas in one faction of the CGT, which contained most of the country's larger unions. A small faction of extremist-oriented Peronistas joined with the Communists, some Socialists, and miscellaneous other labor leaders to form the rival CGT group.

Most Peronistas continued to be united by the end of 1968. It seems likely that with the death of Perón and the return to constitutional government, Peronismo will emerge as the country's principal labor party and the major element in the Argentine democratic left.

The Catholic-oriented Parties

After the fall of Perón, several parties professing to find inspiration for their political program in Catholic social doctrine emerged. Two of these were of some importance in the general political picture of post-Perón Argentina.

The first of these parties was the Christian Democratic Party. Preliminary steps toward establishing this organization were taken more than a year before the fall of Perón and were one of the factors provoking the violent quarrel between the Perón government and the Church in the latter months of 1954. In the 1957 election for a constitutional assembly the Christian Democrats emerged as the fifth largest political group in the country, behind the Peronistas, Popular Radicals, Intransigent Radicals, and Socialists.

During the Frondizi regime, the Christian Democratic Party experienced a split centering on the issue of how the Peronistas should be dealt with. The original leaders of the party were unswerving anti-Peronistas, and rejected the idea that their party should make overtures to the followers of the fallen dictator. They lost control of the Christian Democratic Party to a younger element, which was willing to mute the party's early anti-Peronista stance. During the election of 1963 many Christian Democrats favored the idea of forming a broad united front with the Peronistas, the followers of Arturo Frondizi, and other elements who were in opposition to the principal parties participating in that poll.

The second Catholic-oriented party was the Unión Federal (Federal Union). It was a party of the extreme Right, which fought almost as much against the Christian Democrats as against non-Catholic groups. Since most other parties were not willing or able to deal with this group, it remained a very small element in the nation's political life.

Also the Communists emerged for a while as a party that obtained publicity but had no great influence. Although the party had split during the Perón regime, with one faction backing the dictator and the other opposing him, at least sporadically, the Communists were more or less united in the post-Perón period. They concentrated most of their attention

in these years on wooing the Peronistas and on attempting
to gain influence in the labor movement. However, the great
majority of the Peronistas wanted nothing to do with the
Communists, feeling that their own party and ideology
rivaled Marxism-Leninism. The Communists remained,
therefore, a minority element in the organized labor movement and a small party in the general political picture. In
1967 a small group broke away to form a pro-Peking Communist Party.

Membership and Organization of Parties

All of the important Argentine political parties function
at the national, provincial, and local levels. The grass-roots
organizations, to which the rank-and-file party members belong, carry on a considerable range of activities between
elections: They maintain libraries, conduct classes and lec-
ture series on party philosophy and current events, and hold
public meetings to discuss particular political issues. Some
of these local units publish news bulletins about the party's
national activities, as well as articles of general political
significance. In the larger cities, the more important parties
often have several local headquarters.

Most of the parties also have specialized groups, such as
trade-union committees and youth organizations. In some
parties, women's activities are given special attention. Even
before the advent of woman suffrage, the Socialist Party had
its Unión de Mujeres Socialistas, which conducted a wide
range of activities for women. Later, the Peronistas organized
the Partido Peronista Feminino, which paralleled the all-
male Partido Peronista. (This separation seems to have disappeared since the Peronista parties became illegal in 1965.)
Regular party conventions are held on all levels. At these
congresses, party representatives adopt and amend party programs and change party statutes. In most cases, they also
nominate party candidates for public office. The Socialist

Party, however, nominates its candidates for the Congress, the state legislatures, and municipal offices by membership referendum.

For many years, the Radicals have permitted organized factional groups within their party. These factions, like the party itself, have a complete hierarchy and often maintain their own national and local headquarters. As a result, extensive maneuvering among the factions has often been a dominant feature of the Radical Party congresses. Although the other parties have officially frowned on such factional activity, they have not been immune to internal dissension.

Within the larger parties, patronage has been an important cohesive force. Parties in power can promise or deny their members important government posts—a powerful tool for keeping the rank and file in line with the party leadership. Even opposition parties have a limited degree of control over their members, promising or withholding candidacies for offices that the party has a reasonably good chance of winning.

Although patronage is widespread, corruption has not been the problem in Argentine politics that it has been in some other Latin American countries. Corruption was undoubtedly at its peak during the Perón period, since the President and his wife provided a notorious example of the use of public office for private profit.

It would be impossible to estimate accurately exactly how many Argentines are active in various party organizations. Only the Socialist Party has kept a precise record of the number of its dues-paying members. During periods of intense political activity—the early Perón period and the years between the overthrow of Perón and the ousting of Frondizi —participation in party activities greatly increased. During the administration of President Arturo Illia, however, many party members and citizens who previously had been active in politics became disillusioned with the political system. Al-

though Illia's administration represented the restoration of
party government (in this case, by the Unión Cívica Radical
del Pueblo), after a fierce struggle among the military over
relinquishing national control to the civilian politicians, the
Radical government was unable to resolve any of the country's economic problems or to make any real progress in inte-
grating the Peronistas into the general framework of national
politics. Despite the administration's earnest efforts to incorporate the Peronistas into the political scene, the determination of both military and civilian anti-Peronistas to prevent the Peronistas from achieving any political power was
too strong.

As a result, widespread feelings of frustration and hope-
lessness developed among many politicians because of their
inability to achieve a stable democratic regime. The rank-
and-file citizens, in turn, lost their faith in the party leaders.
Consequently, General Juan Carlos Onganía met with little
resistance from the party chiefs and the general citizenry
when he dissolved all political parties soon after he took
office in June, 1966.

Outlawing of Parties by Ongania

With the outlawing of all political parties by the military
government of General Juan Carlos Onganía in mid-1966,
which made clear its determination to stay in power for
ten years, the quarrels among the various Argentine political
parties were submerged, temporarily at least. It is too early
to say what form the political parties will take if the Onganía
government or its successor once again allows parties to be
organized.

The official banning of the political parties did not in fact
completely end their activities. Although the parties' headquarters were seized and closed and party records were con-
fiscated, the former national leaders of the various parties
continued to meet from time to time and to issue statements

about the current state of affairs. To some degree, the same thing happened on the provincial and local levels. The skeleton organizations of the various groups were thus kept in existence, awaiting the time when the government would again allow the reconstitution of legal parties.

Political Activity of the Military

Meanwhile, even though no political parties formally exist, the many pressure groups that have in the past exerted influence on the country's political life and government continue to function. The most powerful of these interest groups is the military. Ever since 1930, it has been in the foreground of national politics, and in June, 1966, it took full responsibility for running the government and announced its intention to keep this responsibility for a long period of time.

Since 1930, the Argentine armed forces have frequently taken it upon themselves to make and unmake governments. Of the fifteen presidents since 1930, nine have been generals. Even those who were not, have been able to maintain themselves in power only so long as they had at least the tolerance of the military leaders.

This control of political life by the military since 1930 is in sharp contrast to the behavior of the armed forces in the fifty years before that date. Between 1880 and 1930, there was only one military president, Julio Roca, and during his two terms, there was no indication that military pressure had had anything to do with his coming to power. During that half century, the Argentine armed forces were an exemplary exception to the too prevalent tendency of the Latin American military to interfere in politics.

Undoubtedly, certain attitudes of the Argentine military have conditioned them to intervene in politics during recent decades, although in each instance in which they overthrew a government there existed specific reasons for their intervention. They regard themselves as exceedingly patriotic, and they have been suspicious of the patriotism of many of the civilian political leaders since 1930. They also regard themselves as honest and have suspected many of the civilian leaders of being corrupt. They are defenders of law and order, and have often suspected political leaders of being subversive. Finally, they have had a technical training which has led many of the military officers to believe that they are particularly capable of resolving the country's problems, and the failure of their frequent efforts to do so has not dissuaded them from this belief.

Perhaps the fact that the Argentine armed forces have had little occasion to carry out the activities that are the supposed reason for their existence—that is, to protect the national frontiers—has also contributed toward their willingness to take on other, more extraneous functions. Argentina has not fought a war since the conflict with Paraguay in the 1860's. Its frontier incidents, principally with Chile, have been relatively few. Such imperialistic ambitions as some Argentine rulers may have had have not found a military expression.

Although seldom called upon to perform their fundamental task, the Argentine armed forces have traditionally been sizable in numbers and have consumed a large proportion of the government's budget. In 1965, there were approximately 80,000 men in the army, of whom 60,000 were conscript enlisted men,* 5,000 were officers, and 15,000 were professional noncoms. In addition, the country had about 250,000 men in its trained reserves. The army consisted of four army corps made up of five infantry brigades, two mountain brigades, one airborne brigade, and two armored brigades.

The Argentine Navy has some 2,300 officers and 31,000 men, of whom 15,000 are conscripts. Included among the

---

* All men reaching the age of eighteen are eligible for conscription for one year's military service. The relatively small proportion of those eligible who actually serve are chosen by a lottery system.

officers are 250 pilots in the Naval Air Service, organized into four wings. The ships in the Argentine Navy include the 14,000 ton aircraft carrier *Independencia,* formerly belonging to Great Britain under the name *Warrior,* which Argentina acquired in 1958. In addition, there are the cruisers *General Belgrano, Nueve de Julio,* and *La Argentina,* as well as nine destroyers, two submarines, and various lesser craft.

The air force is the youngest of the Argentine armed forces. It has some five air brigades and includes within its ranks some 300 pilots. It has 150 operational aircraft, some of which are jet propelled.

Specific Reasons for Military Intervention

Specific political situations have usually served as reasons or excuses for particular military incursions into politics. In 1930, it was the inability of Irigoyen to deal adequately with the problems provoked by the Great Depression, plus the Conservative and anti-Personalist Radical sympathies of some of the leading officers. In 1943, it was the fear of the pro-Axis Argentine Army leadership that President Ramón S. Castillo was going to impose a pro-British rancher as his successor. In 1955, several provocations pointed to the overthrow of Perón: there were his supposed national betrayal by agreeing to permit the Standard Oil Co. of California to have a concession; his bitter quarrel with the Church; his allegedly excessive favoritism shown to organized labor; the rumored intention to arm his labor supporters; and his growing contempt for many of his military colleagues.

The three post-Perón coups against Presidents Lonardi, Frondizi, and Illia were all motivated to a greater or lesser degree by the military leaders' antipathy for Perón. In the case of Lonardi's overthrow, there was opposition to his conciliatory policies toward the Peronistas, and in the latter two cases, there was fear that the government they overthrew was following policies that would result in the return of the fallen dictator.

Advocates of "Return to the Barracks"

At various times, there have been military leaders who have felt that the armed forces should "return to the barracks" and get out of politics. General Pedro Eugenio Aramburu, president in 1955–58, was one of these. Upon his retirement from the presidency, Aramburu addressed his fellow soldiers and admitted with rare frankness that most of the responsibility for the unsatisfactory progress of their country rested with the members of the armed forces. He stressed that participation in politics was not the appropriate occupation for military men and urged that they leave the running of the government to civilians.

During most of the Frondizi regime, Aramburu used his influence against any attempt to oust the president. However, in the crisis of March, 1962, even he joined with his opponents in the armed forces to move against Frondizi, apparently in temporary panic because of the very good showing made by the Peronistas in the March, 1962, election.

Another post-Perón military leader who was for some time an advocate of the armed forces' remaining in the political background was General Juan Carlos Onganía. Leader of the "Blue" element in the army, he insisted on a return to constitutional government through elections after the ouster of Frondizi in 1963. However, in June, 1966, he led the forces that overthrew President Illia, who had been elected in 1963.

The fact was that the habit of military intervention in politics, which was already deeply ingrained by the time of Perón's overthrow, has been exceedingly hard to break. Perhaps the lesson of this situation is that once constitutional rule has been broken, it gets easier on each succeeding occasion to break it again.

Factions in the Armed Forces

As a result of its political activities, the military, and particularly the army, which normally has been predominant in determining the armed forces' role, has been split into rival factions, which almost resemble parties. These have changed in the course of time, but they have always been present. During the 1930's, there were notable Radical, Anti-Personalist, and Conservative divisions in the army. During the Perón era, and for some time thereafter, the armed forces were split unalterably between Peronista and anti-Peronista groups. During the Frondizi period, there emerged the "Blues," generally sympathetic to constitutional government, and the "Reds," advocating a military dictatorship of unspecified duration. During the Illia period, the same fundamental split continued; the "Reds" became known as the Nasserites and as outright advocates of the military assuming complete control over the government on the unlikely proposition that only they could solve the country's accumulated problems. Although all military factions united in the move to oust the Illia government, the deep divisions of opinion have undoubtedly continued.

The political activity of the military also intensified the natural rivalries among the different armed services. Such conflicts occur in virtually every nation, and they are perhaps more intense in Argentina than in many other countries because of the different backgrounds of the various services; the army was for a number of years under the instruction of a German training mission, whereas the navy was long under British tutelage.

The involvement of the armed forces in politics made interservice rivalries take on the form of armed conflict on a number of occasions in recent years. The navy, with the assistance of a part of the air force, made an unsuccessful attempt to oust the Perón regime in June, 1955, when Perón was saved by a united army command. In September, 1962, the navy constituted the core of an unsuccessful attempt to seize power. During this conflict, naval aircraft attacked a group of army tanks, and the army ultimately captured the main navy base near Bahía Blanca by storm.

Organized Labor as a Pressure Group

Since the early 1940's, the trade-union movement has been the most significant civilian pressure group in Argentine political life. Organized labor grew slowly during the first four decades of this century. However, during the first three or four years of the Perón era, starting with the *coup d'état* of June 4, 1943, the labor movement increased in numbers from about 350,000 to around 2 million members. Virtually all industrial workers, transportation employees, bank clerks, commercial employees, and a considerable number of agricultural workers were brought into the unions.

The new-found strength of the trade unions became evident even before Perón became president. In October, 1945, when Perón was temporarily ousted from his positions in the military government of that time, Perón's trade-union followers, largely organized and led by the chief of the packing-house workers, Cipriano Reyes, declared a national general strike. Hundreds of thousands of union members descended upon Buenos Aires, practically seizing control of the city's streets. Their rioting and demonstrations in favor of the deposed Perón were ultimately responsible for convincing the military men who had ousted him to bring him back.

Not only did the labor movement greatly increase its membership under Perón's influence, but it also became highly centralized. Almost all unions were forced into a single central labor body, the Confederación General del Trabajo (CGT). Similarly, those national industrial unions that had previously enjoyed a decentralized form of organization were now reorganized and the most effective power was lodged in their national headquarters.

So long as Perón was president, he relied heavily on the organized labor movement. He used strikes as a means of keeping many employers in line who were antagonistic to his regime. He continually threatened all military men who wavered in their loyalty to the government with a repetition of the events of October, 1945. On occasion, the Perón government even used certain armed trade-union activists to intimidate opponents of the regime.

Although Perón attempted during his presidency to deprive the labor movement of all freedom of action and to make it merely a tool of his administration, he only partly succeeded in his efforts. After Perón was overthrown, organized labor remained one of the major power factors in Argentina's political structure. Although the unions had little freedom of action during most of the period in which the Aramburu government kept them under the control of military officers, they were once again largely under the control of elected officers by the time Aramburu left office on May 1, 1958.

In the post-Perón period, the labor movement did not abandon its habit of intense political activity established under Perón. Once the majority of the unions were again under Peronista control, they stood as a permanent challenge to each succeeding government. On many occasions, the Peronista labor leadership called the workers out on essentially political general strikes. Although not all of these movements were successful, they did demonstrate a wide degree of solidarity, particularly among the unions in the key industrial ring in and around Buenos Aires. They made all of the governments in power between 1958 and 1966 try to avoid an open showdown with the organized workers, since it was not at all clear whether any regime could survive such a test.

The government of General Juan Carlos Onganía, which came to power by a *coup d'état* in June, 1966, also at first respected the strength of the labor movement. Both Peronista factions in the unions were represented at the ceremonies in which he took the oath of office as president. For a little over six months, there was a kind of honeymoon between the Onganía government and organized labor. However, by early 1967, when it became evident to the union leaders that the Onganía regime had no program to deal effectively with inflation and other economic problems facing the workers and the nation, relations between labor and the administration cooled. Finally, when the leadership of the CGT called a general strike early in 1967 as a first step of a campaign to gain a general wage increase and labor representation in the determination of economic policy, the Onganía government reacted with a strong crackdown on the most militant unions. Thereafter, organized labor's influence decreased significantly. Early in 1968, a split in the CGT, obviously encouraged by the Onganía government, further weakened the labor movement.

The Roman Catholic Church as a Pressure Group

The Roman Catholic Church is another pressure group of considerable significance. Its importance is written into the constitution, which prescribes that the president must be a Catholic and that the Catholic Church is the established church. In spite of these constitutional provisions, the government tended to have an anticlerical cast for sixty years, in 1884–1944. Laws passed in 1884 provided that religion could not be taught in the public schools, that civil marriage was required (religious ceremonies were permitted), and that the control of cemeteries and the collection of vital statistics should be transferred to the state.

The great majority of the Argentine population is at least nominally Catholic. When the military group that seized power in June, 1943, sought to rally civilian support, it attempted to gain the backing of the Catholic Church. To this end, it repealed the laws of 1884 and reinstituted Catholic religious instruction in the public schools. This and other overtures to the hierarchy succeeded in winning the support of most Argentine bishops and clergy for Perón's presidential candidacy in 1946. A pastoral letter was issued by the bishops shortly before that election, saying that no good Catholic could vote for any party supporting separation of Church and state, divorce, or birth control. Since all of the parties in the opposition to Perón supported one or the other of these measures, Perón was, by process of elimination, the only candidate for which, according to the pastoral letter, good Catholics could vote.

The Church again endorsed Perón in the election of 1951. However, by that time, considerable opposition to the regime had begun to develop within the Church, and by 1954, an open conflict had developed between the regime and the Catholic hierarchy. The apparent reason for this was that lay elements associated with the Church tried to establish an active faction in the labor movement, while other middle-class Catholics had organized a Christian Democratic Party. Perón and his associates apparently feared that these two developments constituted a serious menace to his control of the workers, many of whom were as good Catholics as they were good Peronistas.

On the Peronista side, this conflict resulted in the removal of Catholic instruction from the school curriculum by the administration. The regime also passed a law that legalized divorce and another one that legalized prostitution. On yet another level, Peronista mobs burned a number of important Church buildings in Buenos Aires.

The Church retaliated by excommunicating Perón after he had ordered two priests deported. It also organized a massive procession on Corpus Christi day, 1955, although the government had forbidden this. The procession was used as a vehicle for an antigovernment demonstration by virtually all elements opposed to the regime; even agnostic and atheist Socialists, Radicals, and Communists marched in the procession.

This feud between the government and the Church was undoubtedly of great significance in bringing about the overthrow of the Perón regime. Thereafter, the Church continued to exercise considerable influence in the country's politics. The post-Perón regime repealed the Peronista laws that had authorized divorce and prostitution. In the election of 1958, Arturo Frondizi courted Church support by promising to legalize the establishment of Catholic universities. He did carry out this promise soon after taking office. Today, the Church remains a force to be reckoned with in Argentine politics.

The Rural Landlords and Industrialists

Another traditional pressure group, which still continues to have some political influence, is the rural landlord group. Their ranches and farms still produce most of the country's exports. They have influence in the Church and among the officers of the armed forces, and at least some of them still consider reasonable the old argument that Argentina is predestined to be a meat and grain producer and little else. This influence of the landlords was reflected during the Aramburu administration, which took measures to favor them and reversed Perón's policy of giving special consideration to industry.

Also the industrialists exercise considerable influence in politics. Their argument that industry is important for Argentina to have a more balanced economy, less subject to pressures from abroad, finds a ready response among the more nationalist-minded military men. On many issues of economic policy, the industrialists can also find real allies in the organized labor movement.

During the Perón regime, a large part of the industrial class was friendly toward the government, in spite of the regime's favoritism for the working class. This was both because they felt that Perón was the only leader who could keep the labor movement under control and because of the financial backing and tariff protection that the Perón government gave to manufacturing firms. The industrialists also supported Frondizi because he showed enthusiasm for developing industry.

The Intellectuals and the Press

Two other interest groups are of considerable significance, namely, the intellectuals and the press. Intellectuals played an important part in keeping alive the opposition to the Perón dictatorship. Both university faculty and students carried on a running battle with the regime, and Perón retaliated by reorganizing the universities on several occasions. Many important intellectuals went abroad, from where they were very active in keeping the abuses of the dictatorship before world public opinion. A group of young intellectuals, gathered around Arturo Frondizi, played an important role in developing his program for national economic development. Subsequent to the establishment of the Onganía regime, in mid-1966, Onganía's attack on the university was one of the first moves to arouse widespread protest against the new government.

The importance of the press as an influencer of public opinion and as a wielder of political power has been recognized by all recent governments. Perón went to extreme lengths to control the press, through buying up, suppressing, and confiscating publications that were hostile to him. On the other hand, the Aramburu regime dismantled the publishing empire that Evita Perón had built up, selling its various components to private entrepreneurs and political groups. Only during the last months of his administration did Aramburu permit the reappearance of some Peronista-inclined weeklies. With the seizure of power by General Onganía, he immediately took steps to establish censorship of the press.

For its part, the Argentine press has used every opportunity to exercise its right of being critical of the regime in power. Since 1958, the newspapers and magazines published in the country have represented virtually every active political group.

Summary and Conclusion

The average Argentine citizen has a high degree of political consciousness. He is likely to have emphatic opinions on issues facing the country and perhaps will have a strong allegiance to one or the other of the country's political parties. He will often try to make his feelings known, not only through discussion and action but also through participation in a group that can influence the country's government and politics. However, in spite of the concern with politics of the average citizen, it is in the nation's politics that the basic cause of the lingering crisis is to be found. The political leaders have been unable to unite a majority of the people.

The result has been a high degree of political instability, with the military playing the key role in making and unmaking governments.

V

People and Society

Argentines have a touchiness and pride unequaled anywhere in the hemisphere. Yet, for over three decades, the country has been undergoing a social crisis that has affected not only the political and economic spheres but even the cultural.

The Early Population

A vast change occurred in the ethnic composition of the country in the latter part of the nineteenth century and the early years of the twentieth. The Indian-European mixed population that predominated at the time of independence was swamped in the five decades following 1880 by a vast stream of immigrants from southern and Central Europe. The impact left by this clash of cultures and societies has never been fully resolved.

Most of the Indians who lived in Argentina before the Europeans came were primitive hunters and fishermen. Only in the extreme western and northern parts of the country and along the present frontiers with Paraguay and Brazil did there live sizable numbers of Indians who were settled agriculturalists. During the first two or three centuries of Spanish penetration of Argentina, there appears to have been an Indian invasion of the great plains of the pampas from over the mountains in Chile. The warlike Araucanians came over the Andes to conquer the relatively peaceful earlier inhabitants, and it was they who continued to battle

with the Spaniards, and later with the Argentines, for control
of the pampas. Where the Indians practiced agriculture and
were relatively pacific, the Spaniards could impose serfdom,
as they had done in Peru and Bolivia. Elsewhere, an intermittent but continuing state of war existed between the two
groups. Only in the 1880's were the Indians of the pampas
finally subdued.

The process of racial mixture began very early. Indeed,
the Spaniards who came down from Asunción to refound
Buenos Aires in the late sixteenth century were themselves
largely mestizo, that is, children of Spanish fathers and Indian mothers. It was several generations, before Spanish
women came to the area. But by this time, the process of
mixing the blood of the conquerors with that of the conquered was already well advanced.

Throughout the colonial period, Spanish and Indian mixing continued, and to an increasingly large degree, the mestizo
and Spanish groups tended to become a single society. In the
late seventeenth and early eighteenth centuries, many Spanish
artisans or small merchants settled in Argentina, since, by
this time, most of the land in the conquered areas had already been apportioned. These new Spanish settlers, who
were of relatively humble origins, had little to differentiate
them from the mestizos who were also craftsmen and petty
merchants, and they tended therefore to merge into a single
group. The mestizo sons and daughters of the richer Spaniards were recognized by their fathers and became members
of the upper classes of the colonial society.

With the establishment of the Viceroyalty of the Río de la
Plata in 1776, the *criollos* (people of Spanish descent born in
America) and the mestizos had an even greater reason to
form a common front since they were both excluded from
all positions in the new administration, which favored Euro-
pean-born Spaniards. Some people have argued that it was
this sudden imposition of an outside authority on a society

that had long been accustomed to being left alone and running its own affairs that formed the basis for the later revolt against all Spanish control.

A third element in the colonial population was represented by the Negroes and mulattoes. Since the early Spanish conquerors had not come to America to work, and since the Argentine Indian did not, for the most part, submit readily to slavery or serfdom, the Spaniards soon began to import slaves from Africa. During several centuries, the illicit slave trade through ·Buenos Aires was one of the most lucrative branches of smuggling, constituting the most important occupation of that port city.

By the end of the colonial period, Argentina had a very polyglot population. The total number of people in the area was estimated at between 500,000 and 600,000. Of these, 60 per cent were Spanish-mestizo, 30 per cent Indian, and 10 per cent Negro-mulatto. During the following half century, the only major change in this racial balance was the virtual disappearance of the Negro-mulatto group, a phenomenon that still puzzles researchers in Argentine history. It is probable that a fair portion of the male population was forced into the Argentine armies that went across the Andes to liberate Chile and Peru from Spanish control and never returned to Argentina. Most of the remaining Negro-mulatto group was apparently absorbed within a few generations into the population. Today, the largest estimate of Negro-mulatto people in the Argentine population encountered by this writer has been 5 per cent, although this group probably makes up a considerably smaller proportion of the more than 20 million present inhabitants of Argentina.

In mid-twentieth-century Argentina, the ethnic types characteristic of the independence period are found only in the northern parts of the republic; north of the city of Córdoba, the Indian admixture in the population becomes increasingly evident. Aside from small groups of Indians who live largely isolated from the bulk of the population, even in the northern provinces, and aside from the sizable number of Indian migrants from Bolivia and Paraguay who also live in these provinces, a substantial proportion of the native population of the north is mestizo, although thoroughly integrated into the predominantly southern European cultural cast of Argentina.

The Immigrants

As the Indians of the pampas and Patagonia were being driven off, after 1860, opening up of these areas to the growing of cereals and cattle and sheep herding, the population of Argentina underwent a profound change. A vast stream of immigrants welled into a great arc extending north and south from the city of Buenos Aires and encompassing all of the pampas, the northern part of Patagonia, and the edges of the Andean foothills.

These immigrants were attracted by the great prosperity that characterized Argentina during the last decades of the nineteenth century. Hundreds of thousands of temporary migrants came to work on the wheat farms in the late spring and returned after the harvest to work in their native Italy and Spain. This they could do because the seasons in Argentina are opposite to those of southern Europe.

In addition to the "swallows," as these migratory workers were called, millions of other people came to Argentina to stay. Although many, if not most of these, came in the hope of making a fortune and then returning to their native countries, the great majority never succeeded in fulfilling this objective. Instead, they settled in Argentina and returned home only for an occasional visit, if at all. They became the forebears of most of today's Argentines.

Many immigrants would have been delighted to build a homestead as millions of Europeans were doing in North America during the same period; but only a very small number was able to do so, because at the time of the massive immigration in the 1880's, most of the rich agricultural and grazing land had already been apportioned among a small number of landholders. The only status the newly arrived Italians or Spaniards could acquire in the rural society of central Argentina was that of tenant farmer or wage laborer.

There was another factor that militated against the settling of large numbers of immigrants in the rural areas of Argentina: The principal rural products of Argentina were of such a nature or were produced in such a manner as not to demand very large quantities of labor for growing and harvesting. The large cattle herds on the pampas required a relatively small group of cowboys to ride herd on them, and the sheep in Patagonia necessitated even fewer shepherds. In the case of the grain fields of the northern pampas, relatively modern methods of sowing, cultivating, and harvesting were introduced quite early, and labor needs were relatively modest.

As a result of these circumstances, a large proportion of the immigrants who had come to Argentina during the last decades of the nineteenth and the early part of the twentieth centuries settled in the cities. There, many of them became artisans, either running their own shops or working for fellow countrymen who owned small workshops. Some found employment in the packinghouses, granaries, and flour mills that grew up around Buenos Aires, Rosario, and other coastal cities. From World War I on, they worked in the textile mills, shoe factories, oil-processing plants, and cement factories, which began to appear in increasing numbers.

But there were other forms of economic activity that became important sources of employment for the European immigrants. They could engage in the service trades or the small commercial enterprises that proliferated throughout the growing cities, and they could go into the construction business, booming with immigration itself. Immigrant neighborhoods became a general characteristic of the great cities of Argentina, and innumerable groceries, barbershops, bakeries, cafes, restaurants, and similar establishments popped up, in which the newly arrived Europeans could find work. Likewise, the large number of immigrants acted as a major factor not only for bringing about the reconstruction of much of Buenos Aires, Rosario, and other cities, but also for their extension into new areas. For this, the efforts of large numbers of construction workers were required.

Although most of the immigrants were from southern Europe, several important groups came from other parts of the Old World. In the provinces of Entre Ríos and Santa Fé, appreciable numbers of Jewish immigrants from Eastern and Central Europe became agricultural colonists, while thousands of other Jews settled in the larger cities. They became a significant element in the cultural and political as well as in the economic life of the country. Significant numbers of Poles and other Slavs also came to live in the Argentine cities. There were also many thousands of German-speaking immigrants, and even many Frenchmen migrated to Argentina in spite of the general tendency of the French not to leave their motherland permanently. But the small number of British who came to manage or work in enterprises owned by Great Britain had the greatest cultural impact on Argentina, in spite of the fact that they were the group that found it hardest to give up their native language.

For several generations, the organizations established by immigrants played an important part in the cultural and economic life of the major coastal cities. Daily newspapers and other periodicals in Italian, German, Yiddish, English, and other languages had a wide circulation. Mutual benefit societies among the Italians or singing and shooting clubs among the Germans provided important centers of social life and recreation and also helped the immigrants to weather some of the economic storms they had to face in their new country.

The immigrants were assimilated into the life and culture of Argentina with surprising rapidity. There were several reasons for this. First of all, the excellent school system, started during Sarmiento's presidency, made sure that most of the second generation immigrants not only spoke Spanish but were also thoroughly familiar with the geography, history, and the patriotic symbols of Argentina—the flag, the national anthem, the mystique of San Martín and of other national heroes. Another assimilating factor was that most immigrants were Roman Catholics, thus creating no sharp religious conflicts. Even the anticlericalism of many Catholic immigrants tended to echo the anticlericalism already prevalent among the country's elite.

The friendly reception that most Argentines gave the new immigrants unquestionably aided the latter's process of adjustment. The constitution of 1853 gave foreign-born citizens most of the civil rights possessed by native Argentines—only the presidency of the republic was closed to naturalized citizens. In many cases, the immigrants could vote in municipal elections without forsaking their native citizenship. There was also little evidence in those decades of the kind of know-nothingism that, sporadically but importantly, faced the immigrant in the United States. Official policy and the mores of the community tended to welcome the newcomer and to convert him as quickly as possible into a good Argentine.

The second-generation Argentine was usually the staunchest patriot and strongest booster of the land of his birth. He rejected emphatically the foreignness of his parents, refused to learn their language—or learned it only imperfectly—and was ashamed of their mistakes when speaking Spanish. Typically, the sons and daughters of immigrants sought to be more Argentine than those whose ancestors had been in the country for many generations.

The process of assimilation tended to modify the traditional patterns of the country. Buenos Aires and Rosario, and some of the smaller cities, became more European than Latin American in their appearance, with typical Spanish colonial patio-centered houses giving way to the two- or three-story residences usually found in an Italian or French town. The wide avenues made popular in Europe by Napoleon III became characteristic of the coastal cities of Argentina. The cafe, frequently with an extension out on the sidewalk, became focal points of Argentina's principal cities and highly important social centers for the country's male population.

The Argentine-Spanish language was also modified by the impact of immigration. Italian influence was particularly notable, not only in the *lumfardo* patois that was spoken by large numbers of lower-class *porteños* but also in the language of most other Argentines. The soft "g" sound in the pronunciation of the Spanish letters "ll" and "y" and the introduction of many new words, such as the salutation *chou* and the term *che*, used among close friends, were some of the more obvious evidences of the Italian impact.

Italian influence is also reflected in the public behavior of the Argentines. Juan Perón, himself of Italian descent, is perhaps the best example. His florid and expansive style from the balcony of the presidential palace or from thousands of other platforms he occupied during his decade-long domination of Argentine politics were a good deal more reminiscent of Italy than of Spain.

The Porteño-*Interior Conflict*

The large numbers of immigrants in coastal cities, and particularly in Buenos Aires, intensified a fundamental division in the country, which went deep into Argentina's past and related to the split between the *porteños*—the people of Buenos Aires—and the people of the interior. Domingo Faustino Sarmiento underscored this conflict in his famous book

Facundo, subtitled *Civilization and Barbarism,* where Buenos Aires represented the former and the interior the latter.

At least since the middle of the eighteenth century, Buenos Aires had looked outward toward Europe. Its population contained a larger number of people of pure European ancestry than did the rural areas or even the cities of the interior, and there was always a sizable foreign-born population in Buenos Aires.

This contrast between the port and the interior had cultural, economic, and political repercussions. Buenos Aires tended to ape the latest European fashion, whether in ideas, dress and manners, or political institutions. By contrast, the interior emphasized the American rather than the European heritage. It also rebuffed anticlericalism and other ideas originating from the Enlightenment, the French Revolution, or from subsequent events.

This cultural contrast between the coastal area and the interior was noticeable in many ways. For example, the tango, of mestizo and perhaps even Negro origin, and now universally recognized as Argentina's national dance, found no favor in Buenos Aires' society until it had first become popular in the salons of Europe. Even in religion, there were sharp contrasts, people of the interior being much more given to saint worship and the syncretism of Roman Catholicism and Indian and mestizo paganism.

Economically, too, there was a conflict. Over the centuries, the interior towns and cities had developed important handicraft industries which supplied their hinterland. Naturally, these towns wanted to protect these sources of livelihood for their own people, whereas Buenos Aires was interested in importing goods and selling them all over the country. With the rise of the meat and grain economy of the pampas and of Patagonia, more and more parts of the interior became incorporated in the economy of Buenos Aires and of the outside world. Only in Tucumán (and to a lesser degree in Santiago del Estero), where sugar became the main source of income, and in Mendozà, where grape growing and wine-making assumed a major role, did the interior areas develop any production for the national market that could take the place of the handicraft industries that were being destroyed by the flood of imports accompanying the growth of the country's major exports.

Politically, too, there were sharp differences between the interior and the coast. From the earliest days of independence, the city of Buenos Aires and much of its hinterland tended to favor a highly centralized form of government, in which the leading role would be played by the capital. The interior, on the contrary, had long favored federalism, in which each province would have the widest possible latitude to determine its own destiny. This struggle continued through the first three quarters of the nineteenth century, and it was not until 1880, that a compromise was struck, in which the city of Buenos Aires became a federal district and the principle of federalism was formally accepted by the nation as a whole. Ironically, thereafter it was honored more in the breach than in the observance.

The political parties also reflected the *porteño*-interior struggle. The Conservatives, who ruled from the 1860's until 1916, were open Europeanizers, anxious, for cultural as well as economic reasons, to have large-scale immigration and to mold Argentina as an essentially European country. The Socialists, too, many of whose leaders were foreign-born, were determined to recast Argentine politics in a European form. Only the Radicals represented the influence of the interior. But it was Juan Domingo Perón who spoke most effectively to and for both the man of the interior and the fanatically Argentine sons of the European immigrants.

In recent decades, several factors have tended to intensify and several to reduce the conflict between the interior and the coast. On the one hand, after the 1930's immigration had diminished to a trickle—although it resumed to some degree after World War II—the immigrants no longer made a major impact on the country. On the other hand, and as a result of the industrialization process of the 1930's and 1940's, there was a mass migration from the interior of Argentina to Buenos Aires and other coastal areas. This migration has continued, even though the rate of industrial development has slowed down drastically. The impact of domestic migration has been intensified by the fact that there were many Bolivians and Paraguayans among the migrants to Buenos Aires, whose ethnic and cultural backgrounds are mestizo or pure Indian.

As for the ethnic composition of Buenos Aires and of other coastal cities, this influx of people from the interior and from neighboring countries meant the presence in these urban centers of larger numbers of people with non-European antecedents. It also meant that the immigrants and their children, who had made up the majority of the population of the coastal region so far, came, for the first time, into personal contact, with the different traditions and attitudes characteristic of the indigenous Argentines.

The migration to the large coastal cities created a wide variety of social and economic problems. It put new pressure on the health and education facilities of the cities; but, most of all, it fomented the development of a ring of shantytown communities in the outskirts of Buenos Aires and other cities, known as the *villas miseria*. Increased pressure was also put on public utilities, transport facilities, and other public services.

Although it seemed for a while that the contrast between the largely European population of the coastal area and the *mestizo* people of the interior would prevail, Argentina's internal migration may in the long run bring a greater degree of national integration than has heretofore existed. The migrants from the interior will increasingly share the urban experience to which the immigrants' sons have long been accustomed, and these experiences will, in time, be reflected in the interior areas. One can expect some modification of the attitudes and outlook of the people of European extraction, while, at the same time, the impact of European-oriented civilization of the coastal cities will increase in the interior.

Class Structure

Immigration also played a large part in making Argentina the most middle-class country in Latin America. The hundreds of thousands of immigrants who became the proprietors of small workshops and stores soon constituted a very large petty-bourgeois element in the population. And even those immigrants who got their first start in the New World as agricultural or wage laborers in workshops and factories were ambitious to see their children rise on the social ladder. Hence, the second-generation Argentine of very humble origins often moved to the white-collar or even to the growing professional class.

There is no doubt that the country's good educational system also contributed a great deal to the growth of the middle class. The teachers became a very important segment of the middle class, and their instruction created the kind of social mobility that made it relatively easy for a family to rise out of the lower class in one generation.

The fairly modern nature of Argentina's agricultural production also worked in favor of the middle class. In the vast central part of the country, from as far north as Tucumán to as far south as the northern part of Patagonia and from the coast west to Mendoza and San Juan, within sight of the Andes, agricultural laborers worked for wages, which, however small they were, brought them into the market. Only on the periphery of the country did there exist areas of subsistence agriculture, which prevented the growth of a large internal market, as is the case in many other Latin American countries. Thus, a large part of the working population was engaged in making and distributing goods for a domestic market.

The high degree of urbanization has also contributed to the spread of the middle class and of middle-class values. Even a large sector of the wage-earning working class, rubbing elbows with members of the white-collar group each day, acquired middle-class tastes and aspirations. If they or their children did not aspire to white-collar status, they wanted at least to enjoy the material comforts of the middle class; and, to a considerable degree, they succeeded.

It has been estimated that the middle class constitutes 40 per cent of the total Argentine population. At its upper levels, the middle class tends to blend into the old aristocracy, and in its lower reaches, it merges with the wage-earning working class. Many self-made industrialists, who started as immigrant artisans, accumulated fortunes equal to, if not exceeding, those of the members of the old landowning oligarchy. Although, perhaps for a generation, they were not accepted as equals by the older upper classes in spite of their wealth, these distinctions have long since begun to disappear. At the other end of the social scale, many members of the lower middle class come from working class homes, and the exact distinction of class barriers has tended to become blurred, particularly as some wage-earning groups have been able to achieve levels of living that are as good as, if not better than, those of the white-collar workers.

But the over-all importance of class lines and class interests has not disappeared in Argentina; it is still very much a reality. The richer members of the old aristocracy as well as many of the newer rich, have exceedingly elegant homes in the finer residential areas of Buenos Aires, in its suburbs, or in some of the larger provincial cities, as well as residences on their *estancias*. These houses are usually luxurious and show a formality of manners that surpasses almost anything likely to be found in the United States.

The members of the upper class travel frequently to the United States and to Europe; they collect art treasures; they breed fine race horses; they endow the Church; and their wives preside over the country's principal charitable organizations. One of the greatest grievances that this class had against the Perón regime was that it suppressed many of these charitable endeavors and substituted for them the state-run Eva Perón Welfare Foundation, to which the wealthy were forced to contribute.

At the other end of the social scale, the rural poor in the more outlying parts of the country, as well as the residents of the *villas miseria,* live in a degree of poverty and misery that rivals that of the lower classes of poorer Latin American countries. They form the *lumpenproletariat* among which Perón found some of his most fanatical and loyal followers.

During the Perón period, the working class assumed a social and political importance it had never enjoyed before. Perhaps the most significant element in Perón's politics was that, for the first time, he gave the urban and rural working class the feeling that they were full-fledged members of Argentine society. Whatever his motives, it is a fact that Perón made the blue-collar workers of the city and the rural peon feel a kind of dignity, self-esteem, and importance they had never experienced before.

Since Perón, the Argentine working class has been very well organized. During his domination of national affairs, the membership of the Argentine labor movement increased nearly ten times. Collective bargaining became the framework within which relations between workers and employers were handled, even in many rural areas. National or regional collective agreements regulated wages as well as working hours and conditions, while a complicated grievance procedure was developed to handle the problems arising between individual workers and their employers. Under Perón, the Ministry of Labor played an important part in these matters, and the system of collective bargaining was also supplemented by a hierarchy of labor courts that dealt with labor matters and social legislation.

One of the most important aspects of the development of labor relations during the Perón period was the extension of collective bargaining even into the rural areas. Strong unions were organized among the sugar and vineyard workers, and a general labor group was established among the grazing and agricultural workers of the pampas. These groups negotiated and reached collective agreements with the employers. The position of the rural workers was also reinforced by legislation that extended many labor laws, originally enacted for the cities, to the rural areas. These included provisions for an eight-hour working day and for the extension of social security to rural workers.

The Perón period was also characterized by an extension of the legal protection for both urban and rural workers. Elaborate factory laws, designed to protect the worker on the job, as well as comprehensive social-security legislation, providing retirement benefits and health insurance, were enacted. Paid vacations, legal holidays, and year-end bonuses were other benefits of Peronista social legislation.

The Perón period also made the organized-labor movement one of the principal forces in Argentine politics. At least until Juan Carlos Onganía became president, in 1966, all post-Perón regimes sought to avoid an open showdown with organized labor. The leaders of the country's major trade unions were, almost by definition, important political figures, while the bulk of the labor movement remained the core of the Peronista force in national politics.

All of these factors tended to reduce the distinctions between the laborer and the lower middle class. Nowhere was this made more evident than in the increase of vacation and recreation resorts established by various unions for their members. Although a few groups of workers, such as the railroaders and municipal employees, enjoyed such vacation facilities even before Perón, these benefits became generally available to organized workers during the Perón regime. Large and luxurious hotels were either built or taken over by unions in such favorite vacation areas as Mar del Plata on the seashore and in the mountain resorts in the Province of Córdoba. Workers could go there with their families for a week or two at very low cost and could enjoy vacations that had only been available to members of the upper class before World War II.

The Role of the Roman Catholic Church

Both the Argentines of older stock and of immigrant descent are mostly Roman Catholics, about 93.6 per cent of the present population. However, the Church does not play as large a role in Argentine affairs as so large a percentage of Catholics would seem to imply.

In Argentina, as elsewhere in Latin America, the Church was part of the Spanish colonial administration. However, sparse population and the relatively unimportant position of Argentina in the Spanish Empire contributed to the fact that the Church was not as dominant here during the colonial period as it was farther north, in Peru, Colombia, or Mexico. The Church owned comparatively little land and was fairly poor. The Inquisition in Argentina was lax and a sizable number of heretics settled temporarily, or even permanently, in Buenos Aires, engaging in smuggling, during much of the colonial epoch, the principal source of income of that city.

Many of the leaders of the independence movement were not devout Catholics. People like Moreno and Rivadavia were intellectual children of the Enlightenment and of the

French Revolution; they tended to be anticlerical and thus hostile to the secular influence of the Church. Although, during the Rosas period, religious orthodoxy was more in favor, anticlericalism was restored after the overthrow of the Rosas dictatorship.

The people who led the country into the post-Rosas generations were either irreligious or held their religious convictions lightly. Political figures such as Sarmiento and Alberdi were hostile to the secular influence of the Church and sought to have its activities confined to the spiritual sphere. Although the constitution of 1853 made Catholicism the state religion and provided that all presidents of the republic had to be Roman Catholic, the influence of the Church was greatly reduced after the enactment of the constitution.

In the 1880's, the anticlericals won most of the points for which they had fought. Religious instruction was banned from the public schools and only state-controlled universities were permitted. The state rather than the Church was now responsible for keeping vital statistics on births and deaths, and the cemeteries were put under secular control and opened to the deceased of all faiths.

For fifty years, little was done to modify this situation. Many immigrants from Spain and Italy, although Catholics, were anticlerical, while a minority of newcomers from other parts of Europe were Protestants or Jews. Some immigrants were even violently opposed to the influence of the Church. Thus, the Socialist Party, in which the immigrant groups played a particularly important role, went so far as to expel any member who got married in the Church or who permitted his children to do so.

Although the anticlerical laws of the 1880's seemed to become generally accepted, the issue tended to lose importance. Except among the Socialists, the issue was raised only infrequently during the period between the two world wars. It was not until the military *coup d'état* of June 4, 1943, that

the Church-state issue was again forcefully raised. The
tary regime, seeking to ingratiate itself with the Church,
acted a decree law, in December, 1943, that restored t.
teaching of Catholicism in public schools. Since that time,
the question of what the secular role of the Church should
be in Argentine society has been the subject of bitter, albeit
sporadic, controversy.

Late in 1954, Perón once again suppressed Catholic education in the public schools. But in 1958, the Frondizi administration passed a law authorizing the establishment of Catholic
universities and the recognition of degrees granted by them.
The emergence of a Christian Democratic Party, playing
a minor role in national politics since the fall of Perón,
has also served to keep the issue alive; the same holds true for
the continuing controversy over the divorce issue.

Hence, the Catholic Church remains an important element
in Argentine society. But it is neither as strong nor as dog-
matic in Argentina as it is in other Spanish-speaking countries, such as Colombia, Ecuador, or Spain itself. Nor is the
Argentine Church by any means united on all issues. Many
priests were ardent Peronistas, and most bishops supported
him, at least for a while. But there were also others who were
strongly opposed to Perón. Although virtually all clergy and
most practicing Catholic laymen favored the legalization of
Church universities, no unanimity existed concerning Catholic education in public schools. Also on other social and
economic issues, the Church hierarchy, clergy, and laity are
deeply divided.

The Church lacks homogeneity in still another way. Although the Church in Argentina is more homogeneous and
orthodox in theological and liturgical matters than it is in
Spanish American countries with a large Indian population
or in Brazil, considerable divirgence in these matters still
exists in different parts of the country. In the more remote
parts of Argentina, the Church tolerates liturgical and per-

haps also theological innovations by the local faithful that it
would never allow in Buenos Aires or in other large cities.
In some areas, the old Indian gods are by no means dead but
hide behind Christian saints and the Catholic altar. In these
parts of Argentina where the Indian influence is most marked,
the Catholic Church has demonstrated similar flexibility in
allowing a certain fusion of Catholic hagiography and pre-
Colombian faiths.

Today, Argentina is one of the largest Catholic countries
in the world, ranking in population only after Brazil, Italy,
France, Mexico, and Spain. In 1966, Argentina was represented by two members in the College of Cardinals, one of
whom, Giacomo Luigi Cardinal Copello, held the post of
Chancelor of the Holy Roman Church in the Vatican Secre-
tariat. The second member was Antonio Cardinal Caggiano,
the Archbishop of Buenos Aires.

Other Religious Groups

Although many Argentines who were baptized in the Catholic Church and whom the Church bears on its rolls as members do not consider themselves as such, the membership in
other religious groups is very small. Only 2 per cent of the
population is listed as Protestant and about 2 per cent as
Jewish. Other faiths are virtually nonexistent.

The Protestants are mostly members of ethnic minority
groups, notably Germans. Although some Protestant prosely-
tism has taken place in Argentina, no large indigenous Protestant groups have as yet developed as, for example, in Brazil
and Chile.

The Jews have played a significant role in Argentine life
only in the present century. Buenos Aires is the largest center
of Jewish population in Latin America, and there are Jewish
minorities in other big cities. A prosperous group of Jewish
agricultural colonists lives in the Province of Entre Ríos.

Jews are important not only in the country's economic but also in its cultural and political life. Both the Radical and Socialist parties have had outstanding Jewish leaders.

Although the Jews have generally integrated themselves thoroughly into Argentine society, a strain of anti-Semitism has continued to exist in Argentine politics for nearly four decades. Some of the civilian leaders of the *coup d'état* of September, 1930, were outspoken anti-Semites. During the 1930's, the rise of Hitler intensified this trend, although the Argentine governments of that period were not avowedly anti-Semitic. Anti-Jewish literature, notably the novels of Hugo Wast, enjoyed considerable popularity at that time.

During the early part of the Perón period, some of Perón's followers showed an outspoken anti-Semitic attitude. But Perón himself rejected anti-Semitism and went out of his way to assure the leaders of the Jewish community that he did not share the sentiments and opinions of some of his more raucous subordinates. At least one leading member of the Perón government, Angel Borlenghi, who was Perón's long-time minister of interior, was Jewish.

After the fall of Perón, anti-Semitism revived, particularly on the part of a semi-secret society known as the Tacuara. This society confined itself largely to painting swastikas and anti-Jewish slogans on walls, although there were some instances, where synagogues and individual Jews were attacked. The Tacuara vanished in the early 1960's, but anti-Jewish activities revived again right after the military coup of June, 1966, when President Juan Carlos Onganía hastened to assure the Argentine Jewish leaders and the world that his regime had no connection with these activities.

Although a nuisance and perhaps a source of potential danger, anti-Semitism has never been a major problem in Argentina. Whatever xenophobia the average Argentine may have, he has not been inclined to direct it against his fellow Jewish citizens.

Relations Between the Sexes and Between Generations

Perhaps because of its strongly European background, and because Argentina never suffered to the same degree from semi-feudalism as other Latin American countries with predominantly Indian or Negro populations, Argentina has a more modern attitude toward the relations between the sexes and the position of the young than many other Latin American nations. Although the double standard in marital relations, which seems to be so characteristic of the Latin countries, has also been widespread in Argentina, the Argentine woman has perhaps never been as much subordinated to her husband as women in other Latin American countries.

The double standard still exists in Argentina. The marriage vows are taken very seriously by the wife, but the husband has a great deal of latitude. It is not regarded as particularly scandalous if a man has a *casa chica,* that is, if he maintains a mistress in addition to his legal spouse. It is also considered generally desirable that a young man have considerable sexual experience before marrying; a young woman, however, is expected to go as a virgin to her marriage bed.

Most of the older mores are breaking down though. Several generations have passed since young unmarried men and women in the larger cities and towns were expected to be accompanied by a chaperon when going out in public, even in the most punctilious middle- and upper-class families. Today, it is quite normal to see young couples alone in the streets, in movies, theaters, restaurants and cafes, dance halls, and other public places.

In another way, too, old customs have largely disappeared. Marriage is now a question to be decided largely by the couple involved. Although arranged marriages still occasionally take place among some of the older oligarchical families, they are few and occur seldom.

It has also long been considered proper for a woman—whether married or unmarried—to take a job, and it is likely that the early establishment of an extensive and good-quality school system, largely staffed in its primary grades by women, had a good deal to do with the acceptance of female employment in Argentina. It has been true for many years that a great number of jobs in offices and stores are filled by women. There is also a scattering of professional women, such as lawyers, doctors, or social workers.

Although Argentine women were not allowed to vote until the Perón era, they were quite early conceded the right to own property in their names. In most civil rights, Argentine women now enjoy equality with men.

Argentine women have played a growing but still relatively small role in politics despite the fact that they attend political meetings and rallies in considerable numbers. The Socialist Party pioneered in giving women leadership roles within a political organization, the Unión de Mujeres Socialistas (the Union of Socialist Women), which conducted active agitation and organization among women long before they could vote.

Eva Perón gave a particular fillip to the participation of women in politics. Even before her husband was president, she conducted a highly political radio program. After he became president, she organized the Partido Peronista Feminino. As a result, a sizable number of women were elected to public office during the Perón period. In 1951, Evita Perón was even nominated by the Peronistas for vice-president of the republic, but was forced to decline the nomination under military pressure.

The influence of the Catholic Church is still very much in evidence in at least one aspect of the relations between the sexes: divorce is not legal in Argentina. Although late in his administration, President Perón pushed through a law legalizing divorce against the will of the Church, this measure was repealed after his overthrow. Individuals who wish to get a divorce, and can afford it frequently go to Uruguay or Chile. The status of remarriage and of children born outside of the first marriage is, however, somewhat doubtful.

The Argentine young, too, suffer less strictness and control from their elders than their contemporaries in many other Latin American countries. The chances are very good that they will get a better education than their parents and they can hope to gain a more prestigious position than their forebears. The immersion of most young people in urban life, which is now typical of Argentina, means that it is very difficult for the parents to exercise the kind of control over adolescents that is still prevalent in many parts of Brazil, Mexico, and other Latin American nations.

It is important to note that, because of a comparatively low birthrate, the percentage of adolescents and of the very young in Argentina's population is considerably smaller than in most other Latin American countries. This is perhaps one reason why they have had less impact on the country's political life in recent years, in spite of the long tradition of student political activity, than have young people in much of Latin America.

Argentine National Pride

Argentines of both sexes and all ages have long been characterized by a very marked degree of national pride. People of the neighboring countries have often regarded the Argentines as overbearing and almost supercilious in their assumption that, in all ways, Argentina is superior to the rest of Latin America.

Heightened national pride is nothing new in Argentina. Domingo Faustino Sarmiento commented upon it more than a century ago and lamented its sometimes exaggerated forms. The passage of time and the arrival of millions of immigrants has not changed this facet of Argentina's national character. Indeed, one might, at least in part, explain the exaggerated expressions of pride in the mid-twentieth century Argentina in terms of immigration itself.

A large part of Argentina's population consists—and has consisted for a considerable time—of the children of immigrants. In Argentina, as in the United States, the offspring of immigrants have often been the most vocal advocates of patriotism and exalters of their country's virtues. In part, perhaps, they assume this posture as a reaction to the foreignness of their parents and to their own need to convince themselves and their compatriots that they are really citizens of the New World. Typically, the immigrants' sons and daughters are very boastful about even the most modest accomplishment of their native land.

There have also been some racial overtones to Argentine pride, such as praising the pure European ancestry of most Argentines and, looking down on their neighboring countries with mestizo or Negro populations.

The nature of the Argentine pride is similar to that of his North American counterpart. He is proud of the size of his capital city, of his nation's richness, and particularly of its natural resources. He is convinced of the manifest destiny of his country in the hemisphere, and perhaps in the world. He is sure that the Buenos Aires subway is the finest anywhere on the globe. He takes pride in the lavishness of his diet and in the originality and worldwide popularity of the tango. He is sure that Argentine movies are technically superior to those of Mexico—the only other major producer of Spanish-language films—and in subject matter to those of Hollywood. He takes it for granted that the Argentine armed forces could defeat all likely opponents.

Since the fall of Perón, pride in Argentina's achievements

has tended to be somewhat more muted. Many sensitive Argentines have been both puzzled and ashamed at the apparent failure of their country to find a way out of the alternation between military dictatorship and near-chaos, which has been the nation's lot for more than a generation. They have also been increasingly upset by Argentina's inability to develop its economy adequately. This is particularly true since some other Latin American countries have shown an ability to combine rapid economic development with a considerable political stability. As a result, many Argentines have become less convinced of the superiority of their nation's achievements over those of their neighbors.

Conclusion

The Argentines are one of the most homogeneous peoples in Latin America. They represent a mixture of pre-independence Spaniards and Indians and of the descendants of one of the major waves of immigration that swept over any American nation in the late nineteenth and early twentieth centuries. The achievement of merging these two groups into a single nation is an accomplishment of which all Argentines are rightfully proud.

Several forces have been of key importance in forming the Argentine nation. One element has been the system of public education, which has tended to instill in all Argentines, whatever their origin, a feeling of patriotism and a common body of national history and symbolism. This has resulted in a certain degree of unity in outlook and loyalties. A second element has been the fact that the great majority of both the original Argentines and the immigrants were Roman Catholics. A third force in the growth of national unity has been that virtually all Argentines were drawn into the market economy, as a result of the vast expansion of the grain and meat export industries between 1880 and 1930 and of the subsequent growth of manufacturing. This factor has tended to develop uniformity in tastes and customs.

The chief stumbling block to fuller national unity was and is the class division of the country. The job of fully incorporating the working classes and the large elements of the lower middle class into national life has not yet been completed. Although Perón gave these groups a feeling of self-importance and power they had never possessed before, the bitter controversy, since 1955, over Perón's possible return to power has worked to prevent a consolidated position of the workers and of the lower middle class. Imaginative political leadership will be necessary before such a consolidation can be achieved.

VI

Cultural Activities

During the first four decades of the twentieth century, Argentina was in the vanguard of cultural developments in the Spanish-speaking world. Its people were more literate than other Latin Americans, books published in Buenos Aires were sold wherever Spanish was read, and its newspapers and journals were of hemispheric fame.

During the last three decades, however, Argentina has tended to fall behind in cultural as well as economic and political affairs. Its people have not been able to build upon the initial advantage they possessed, and Argentina no longer occupies the vanguard position in arts and letters that it held a generation ago.

General Education

Argentina has a long tradition of a strong public-school system. It originated during the post-Rosas period and grew particularly during the administration of Domingo Faustino Sarmiento, who was president between 1868 and 1874. Sarmiento was a passionate advocate of education as a means of national redemption and is responsible for the famous phrase "To govern is to educate." During the long years of the Rosas dictatorship, which Sarmiento spent in exile, he had much time to study the educational system in other countries. He spent some time in the United States and became

146

a friend of the famous American pioneer educator Horace Mann.

When Sarmiento became president, he made the organization of a universal system of public education one of his primary goals. For this purpose, he sought the aid of Horace Mann, who, in turn, arranged for the recruitment of a number of U.S. public-school teachers, particularly from New England, to help establish an Argentine public- and, especially, normal-school system. As a result, public-school education was available for most of the urban population by the early decades of the twentieth century. There were even the beginnings of a school system in the smaller towns and in the countryside, although the success of Sarmiento's and those of his successors' efforts were less notable in the country than in the cities.

The result of this development was that, whereas about two-thirds of the population were illiterate in 1869, only one-third of a much larger population was illiterate by 1914. In that year, 80 per cent of the school-age children in Buenos Aires were actually in school. However, in some of the interior provinces, where the educational efforts had been less intense, the proportion of children in school was only about 40 per cent.

The drive to provide all children with a primary education continued after 1914. By the late 1950's, the United Nations Educational, Scientific and Cultural Organization (UNESCO) estimated that, with some 13 per cent, Argentina had the lowest illiteracy rate in all of Latin America.

Education is compulsory, in theory at least, for all Argentine children between the ages of seven and fourteen. Public education is free on all levels, from primary school to university. As in most countries, education in Argentina is divided into the three levels of primary, secondary, and university education. The primary schools last seven years. Thereafter, a student who wants to continue in school has three choices. If he has aspirations to go to the university, he will enter a *colegio,* organized along the model of the French *lycée,* from which he will receive a *bachillerato,* enabling him to enter one of the professional schools on the university level. A second alternative on the secondary-school level is the normal school, which trains teachers for primary-level teaching. As elsewhere in Latin America, most students enter the normal schools directly after leaving primary school. Only institutions training secondary-school teachers are on the university level. A third alternative for a graduating elementary-school student is to enter a vocational school. Schools for specialized training in agriculture and some urban trades were established even before World War I. They were greatly expanded during the Perón period in order to meet the growing need for trained workers in the country's industries. Most Argentine students do not go beyond primary school. Only about 15 per cent attend a secondary school, and only 5 per cent go on to the university.

Issues in Primary and Secondary Education

Several problems have been a chronic source of controversy in Argentine lower and middle education. One of the most pressing problems has been the need to obtain sufficient funds for adequately financing the country's educational needs. Particularly with the onslaught of inflation in the 1950's, there was a chronic tendency for the cost of living to outrun the increases in teachers' salaries, and teachers' strikes were not unknown. The percentage of the Argentine national budget spent for education is one of the lowest in Latin America.

Questions of an ideological nature have also been constantly debated. One of these has concerned the role of the Church in the educational system. By a law of 1884, education was made the principal responsibility of the state, and the Church was forbidden to operate universities. Similarly, religious teaching was removed from the public schools. This law remained in effect for almost sixty years, and only after the army coup of 1943 did the military regime reinstitute Catholic instruction in the public schools. Over a decade later, in 1954, when the Perón administration was quarreling with the Church, religious instruction in the public schools was again forbidden. It has so far not been reinstated.

During most of its existence, the public-school system has been a bastion of liberal thought. Political figures such as Rivadavia, Juan Bautista Alberdi, and Sarmiento tended to be presented in the most favorable light, while Juan Manuel Rosas' career was painted in the darkest colors. With the advent of the Perón regime, this traditional ideological stand of the Argentine public school was vastly altered. Rosas became a great nationalist rather than a tyrant in textbooks and classes, and the school system was used as a means of converting the younger generation to Peronismo.

The Peronista propaganda in the schools went to almost unbelievable extremes. Some of the textbooks used to teach children how to read dealt, for instance, with almost nothing but the supposed accomplishments of Perón's new Argentina and the virtues of the president and his wife, Evita. One such textbook, used after Evita's death, contained a poem picturing the late first lady as a star in the heavens looking down on her beloved Argentina.

With the overthrow of the Perón regime, a sharp reversal in the ideology of the public schools took place. Much time and effort was devoted to devising a democratic curriculum, placing stress once again on the country's liberal traditions and denigrating the military dictators of both the distant and recent past. But there were many teachers who were also dissatisfied with this new orientation of the curriculum.

The University

Argentines have long and rightly been proud of their university system. Its quality was traditionally high, and proportionately more students were in attendance than in any other

Latin American country. However, the universities, like the rest of education, have suffered from the national crisis of the last few decades.

Until the late 1950's, all universities in Argentina were under the control of the national government. For many years, there were six such institutions in Buenos Aires, La Plata, Córdoba, Tucumán, the Litoral (Rosario and Santa Fé), and Cuyo (Mendoza). In recent years, two new national universities have been added, in Bahía Blanca in the southern part of the Province of Buenos Aires and in the northeast.

The Church was for a long time eliminated from the field of higher education. In 1958, the Frondizi government pushed legislation through Congress that allowed the establishment of private universities. Since then, Catholic institutions have been established in Córdoba and in several other cities, and a Protestant-oriented university was officially recognized in Buenos Aires.

Until the end of World War I, the Argentine university tended to be a very conservative institution. Philosophy and the classics were heavily represented in its curriculum, while the physical sciences were given little and the social sciences virtually no emphasis.

In 1918, the University of Córdoba developed what came to be known as the University Reform Movement. The students went on strike and demanded fundamental changes in the curriculum and in the organization of the university. The movement soon spread to other Argentine universities and, in time, to most universities of Latin America. The University Reform Movement sought four basic changes. First, it wanted to modernize the curriculum and to introduce, on a massive scale, both the physical and social sciences. Second, it sought university autonomy, that is, the right of the university to be free from governmental pressure and free to determine its own policies. Third, the movement sought representation of the students in the administration of the university; and, finally, it felt that the university should go out into the community at large, where it should act as a force favoring fundamental social change.

The University Reform Movement won most of its demands in subsequent years. The curriculum was vastly altered; in fact, this process of change is still going on. A large degree of autonomy was given to the university, and the government allowed it to run its own affairs. The students were given equal representation with the faculty and alumni in picking university authorities. On the whole, therefore, the students in particular, tended to act as a force for change within the society at large.

However, the victories of the University Reform Movement were not permanent. During the Perón period, the faculty and student body were the most consistent and persistent opponents of the dictatorship, with the result that many faculty members were dismissed, and the institutions of higher learning were submitted to close control by Perón's Ministry of Education. Although university autonomy was restored after the fall of Perón, the new military dictatorship of General Juan Carlos Onganía issued a Statute of the Universities, in April, 1967, that once again subjected these schools to close supervision by the national government and removed all student representation from the universities' governing bodies.

In addition to the continuing quarrel over nature and organization of the institutions of higher education, the Argentine universities have been faced with many other problems. One of the most urgent is money. Although there was a vast increase in the number of students attending the universities during the Perón period—which continued after Perón—the budgets of the institutions of higher learning were not increased proportionately. As a result, the Argentine universities have, ever since the 1940's, been characterized by overcrowded classrooms, inadequate facilities and equipment, and by a general decline in their ability to do their job. These inadequacies were particularly felt in the medical schools and in other scientific institutions that require expensive equipment and a very high ratio of faculty to students.

Another problem has been that the traditional system of paying the faculty members only token salaries—which is characteristic of all Latin American countries—has proven to be rather inadequate in the face of the growing demands for research and quality teaching in the universities. Some school administrators, such as Risieri Frondizi, who served as rector of the University of Buenos Aires in the late 1950's and early 1960's, sought to extend the number of full-time faculty members. Despite these efforts, however, full-time professors are still a minority on the teaching staffs of the universities.

Another major problem facing the Argentine universities is inadequate buildings. As in most other Latin American countries, the universities in Argentina have been located in ancient edifices scattered around the center of the cities that are utterly inadequate for modern university purposes, such as laboratories, libraries, and other essential elements of a modern institution of higher learning; there are also no dormitories for out-of-town students.

Only in most recent years an attempt has been made to build university cities or campuses that would bring all or most of the constituent parts of a university together in one area. The University of Buenos Aires has a particularly spectacular plan for such a campus; although started, it has been seriously hampered by inadequate funds.

A final major problem facing Argentine universities is the so-called brain drain, since there is a strong tendency among Argentine intellectuals, scientists, and technicians to leave the university and seek employment abroad. In part, this is due to the better economic position they can achieve in other countries, particularly in the United States and in Europe but also in such Latin American countries as Venezuela. An even more important factor, however, has been the continuing political instability, resulting in precarious living conditions for many, particularly for those concerned with social sciences and humanities.

The entire university system was placed in jeopardy in 1966, when the Onganía government sent troops to occupy the University of Buenos Aires. The faculty's reaction to this violence against the University was militant. Over 1,000 faculty members resigned, many of whom went abroad. Because of the strong stand taken by these professors, the government was more cautious in dealing with the universities in the interior.

The Social and Physical Sciences

The high literacy in Argentina, as well as the large number of people who have gone to a university, has helped to stimulate the development of both the social and physical sciences. In the social sciences, Argentine scholarship is perhaps most outstanding in the field of sociology. A refugee from Mussolini's Italy, Gino Germani, took a leading role in stimulating and organizing modern sociological studies, mostly at the University of Buenos Aires. (After the 1966 coup, Germani went to live in the United States.) Younger scholars, such as Torcuato di Tella, have also brought distinction to their country in the field of sociology.

Argentina has produced some economists of note. The most outstanding is certainly Raúl Prebisch. He gained most of his experience in the 1930's when he was president of Argentina's Banco Central. Soon after World War II, he wrote the first serious study in Spanish on the ideas of the great English economist John Maynard Keynes. However, Prebisch's fame is based mainly on his service as Secretary-General of the United Nations Economic Commission for

Latin America. In that post, he developed a series of new approaches to the problem of economic development in underdeveloped countries which made him the principal spokesman for that large group of nations. This role was recognized in 1963 when he left ECLA to become the Secretary of the United Nations Conference on Trade and Development.

Argentine history and philosophy have also had outstanding scholars. Among the historians is José Luis Romero, who has written excellent studies of the European Middle Ages and of his own country's history. Among the country's leading philosophers are Francisco Romero and Risieri Frondizi, the latter a brother of former President Arturo Frondizi.

The universities have contributed much to stimulate the development of the social sciences. In recent years, several private institutions were established, which have been particularly useful in financing social-science research. The most outstanding among these is the Torcuato di Tella Institute, set up by Guido and Torcuato di Tella, who themselves were prominent social scientists and sons of one of the country's pioneer industrialists, Torcuato di Tella, after whom they named their foundation. This foundation became particularly important after the occupation of the University of Buenos Aires by government troops in 1966, since it provided refuge and employment for many of the scholars who had resigned from the University.

The physical sciences have also made some progress in Argentina in recent decades. This progress was recognized in 1947, when Dr. Bernardo Houssay received the Nobel Prize for medicine. In general, however, the physical sciences have suffered from two characteristics of contemporary Argentina: the difficulty of providing sufficient funds for the expensive equipment and the nation's chronic political instability. This became particularly serious in 1966, when, as a result of the attacks by the Onganía government on the universities, an appreciable number of the country's scientists resigned their university posts and left the country.

Publishing and Literature

During the latter part of the nineteenth and the early part of the twentieth centuries, Argentina developed a vibrant and varied artistic and literary life. The booming economy of the period, and the rapid transformation of Argentina from a backwater of the hemisphere into the most dynamic and powerful nation of Latin America undoubtedly contributed to this development.

Very important, too, was the fact that Argentina, and particularly Buenos Aires, became a major publication center for Spanish-language books and periodicals. At a time when few books were published in other Spanish American countries—most of relatively primitive quality anyhow—Buenos Aires' enterprises published works of authors from all over the Spanish-speaking world. From 1900–40, publishing houses such as Peuser, Guillermo Kraft, Editorial Claridad, Editorial Losada, and William Jackson S.A. were famous throughout the hemisphere and were selling books in all Spanish-speaking countries. After the Spanish Civil War, Spanish firms such as Espasa-Calpe moved their headquarters to Buenos Aires, while Spanish refugees started new publishing ventures such as Americalee. These companies served markets not only in Argentina but in other Latin American countries as well.

Argentine newspapers also became an important intellectual influence at home and abroad. They were not only purveyors of news but also carried essays, short stories, poetry, and literary criticism. Among the most notable papers were *La Nación* and *La Prensa,* the deans of the Latin American press, the well-known Socialist daily *La Vanguardia,* and others. In addition, there were numerous weekly and monthly periodicals with a circulation far beyond the nation's frontiers.

The group that dominated the intellectual scene roughly between 1880 and 1910—sometimes called the Generation of 1880—was characterized by two well-defined tendencies: One was to import into Argentina styles and ideas from Europe; the other was to search into the country's own past for inspiration and even form. Among those intellectuals who looked to Europe, French literary influence was particularly strong, and many writers continued to reflect the French Romantic School, which had first been transplanted to the Río de la Plata area by Esteban Echeverría in the first half of the nineteenth century. There were also numerous writers who found their inspiration in the works of such French literary figures as Flaubert, Balzac, and Zola.

European influence was also felt in areas other than belles-lettres. During the early years of the twentieth century, Joaquín González, one of the great architects of the country's public school system, and founder of the University of La Plata, was also famous as a humanistic philosopher. At the same time, Alejandro Korn brought to Argentina the influence of the German philosophers and stressed the importance of the scientific method of investigation in the university. Finally, José Ingenieros, a pioneer in the fields of sociology and history, introduced many of the techniques then prevalent in Europe and undertook many studies still of value.

The other intellectual current prominent in the generation of the 1880's concentrated on Argentina's interior. Perhaps its finest masterpiece is the great epic poem *Martín Fierro* by José Hernández, picturing the sufferings of the gaucho wrenched from his seminomadic life on the pampa to participate in the struggle against the Indians in the south. Other writers chose different aspects of life in the pampas and in the old colonial towns as their themes.

By the second decade of the twentieth century Argentine

literature had gained a position of pre-eminence throughout the Spanish-speaking world and was becoming known even in other parts of the world. James Scobie describes that situation in the following terms:

> Prosperity permitted Argentina the luxury of the arts, and numerous writers, painters, and musicians now devoted themselves primarily to creative efforts. Wealth enabled Argentina to indulge also in introspection and self-criticism, as the generation of 1910 concerned itself with building a national ethos, with problems of social injustice and with self-conscious rebellions against form.*

After 1910, Argentine literature began to show a strong nationalistic tinge. As Scobie points out, two mainstreams developed, one liberal and epitomized by Ricardo Rojas, the historian, essayist, and literary critic, and the other authoritarian, led by Manuél Gálvez, who turned back to Argentina's gaucho-caudillo type for inspiration. The Gálvez trend degenerated in the 1920's and 1930's into pure xenophobia mixed with anti-Semitism and was epitomized by the poor but popular novels of Hugo Wast.

Also the theater gained considerable importance after 1910. Its outstanding figure was Florencio Sánchez, generally considered the best playwright Argentina has produced so far. Argentine novelists, poets, essayists, and critics also flourished between 1910 and 1930. Argentine periodicals and publishing houses also served as a proving ground for young literary hopefuls from other Spanish-speaking countries where the opportunities for literary expression were not as great as in Buenos Aires.

The year 1930 represents the highwater mark of Argentine leadership in the Spanish-speaking world in cultural as in most other affairs. Thereafter, the cultural development of the country seemed to stagnate. After the revolution of 1943,

---

* James Scobie, *Argentina: A City and a Nation* (New York: Oxford University Press, 1964), p. 213.

the stagnation became even more marked. James Scobie has summed up the situation as follows:

> The generation of 1910 matured but few new figures emerged in the 1930's or 1940's to continue the excitement and activity that Buenos Aires had experienced at the turn of the century. Introspection took over as the essayists struggled not only with the question of what Argentina was but also with the problem of what had happened to Argentina. . . . Opera, concerts, lectures, exhibitions, and publishers' lists provided frequent and polished offerings, and porteños complacently prided themselves on a cultural life which they judged unsurpassed in the hemisphere. . . . [Yet] Argentina achieved intellectual maturity only ːo see the rising talents of Mexico and Brazil threaten its leadership of the Latin American intellectual and artistic community.*

The Stage and the Movies

The appearance of a number of outstanding national playwrights undoubtedly helped to stimulate the development of the legitimate theater in Argentina. Despite the turbulent political history of recent decades, which has often entailed strict censorship of the stage as well as of publishing and of other written forms of expression, the Argentines, particularly in Buenos Aires, have continued to show a very lively interest in Argentine and foreign plays. This interest was evident even during the Perón period. Former U.S. Ambassador to Argentina, James Bruce, wrote about the theatrical situation in the early 1950's:

> Buenos Aires has twenty-eight legitimate theaters running in season. Many are centered on or around Corrientes, the Broadway of Buenos Aires. According to a compilation by "Variety," the theatrical weekly, some 115 productions were put on during

* James Scobie, *Argentina*, p. 214. An exception to this general picture of the decline of Argentine literary leadership after 1930 was the appearance, in that year, of the magazine *Sur*, edited by Victoria Ocampo. For the next twenty-five years, it played an important role in publishing young writers from all over Latin America.

the first nine months of 1951. Twenty-four were translations of foreign dramas. Translators, by the way, often get the same billing as authors, and rate just as highly.

Argentine audience reaction is as unpredictable as ours. Successes are sometimes unexpected, as were "Our Town," and "Arsenic and Old Lace," both of which had extensive runs. In 1951, "The Heiress" had a short run, while André Boussin's "Nine," seen briefly on Broadway the same season, ran for 103 performances.*

In spite of the political turmoil of the post-Perón years, Argentine interest in the legitimate theater remained high. During part of this period, the satirical political review, which had been in eclipse during the Perón dictatorship, revived, making fun, sometimes in very sharp terms, of current government and party leaders. Before Perón, this had been one of the most popular forms of stage presentation; it was revived with vigor after his overthrow.

In the allied field of the cinema, the Argentines got an early lead over other Spanish-speaking countries. As early as the 1920's, the Argentines produced some of the first Spanish motion pictures. In later years, Argentina occupied, together with Mexico, virtually a monopoly position in the Spanish movie business.

Argentine films are shown throughout the Spanish-speaking world. Lately, an increasing number has been displayed in New York and in other cities of the United States with a large Spanish-speaking population.

The Argentine movies vary greatly in subject matter, technique, and quality. In general, Argentine films lack the bittersweet quality that so often characterizes Mexican movies, and are for this reason often more popular in Latin America than Mexican movies. They run the gamut from Westerns with gaucho heroes through musicals and whodunits to more serious dramas.

* James Bruce, *The Perplexing Argentines* (New York: Longmans, Green & Co., 1953), p. 227.

Music and Musicians

Traditionally, the cultural life of Argentina has been enriched by high performance standards in both classical and popular music as well as by a great wealth of native creative musical talent. Ever since 1908, the Teatro Colón in Buenos Aires has been one of the great opera houses and concert theaters in the world. It seats 3,500 listeners and is therefore larger than most other great opera houses of the world. Arturo Toscanini began his conducting career in the Teatro Colón, and it has seen and heard the performances of such greats as Caruso, Pavlova, Chaliapin, Artur Rubinstein, and many others.

However, the Teatro Colón is not the only center for the performance of serious music, since during the mass immigration, many groups of newcomers set up their own musical organizations. Among the contemporary groups noted for the quality of their performances are the Wagnerian Association and the Argentine Philharmonic Association.

Argentina has also produced some composers who have won recognition at home and abroad. McKinney and Anderson have discussed these composers in the following terms:

> In the Argentine, the best-known name seems to be that of Juan José Castro, conductor of the Colón opera, Buenos Aires, a brilliant and very successful composer as well as conductor; his brother, a composer of even greater talent, José Mario Castro, is not so well known outside his native country. Juan Carlos Paz seems to have become enamored of Schonbergian twelve-tone ideals, while the young Alberto Ginastera is looked upon by the Argentine musicians as their most promising composer.*

In recent years, Ginastera's operas have received world-wide attention. Ironically, these works were banned by the On-

---

* Howard McKinney and W. R. Anderson, *Discovering Music* (New York: American Book Co., 1943), p. 266.

ganía government, on the grounds that they offended public morals.

Argentine music is best known, however, because it has given the world the tango. Apparently of mixed African, Indian, and European origin, the tango originally became popular in the bistros of the working-class sections of Buenos Aires. The tango was not considered "nice" by the Argentine upper classes until it achieved great popularity in Europe, particularly in Paris. Thereafter, the tango became a source of national pride for Argentines of all classes. To foreigners, the tango has become synonomous with Argentina itself.

The tango is not the only kind of Argentine popular music. In Buenos Aires and in other urban centers, waltzes written by Argentine composers rival the tango in popularity. Both compete with various types of American jazz which is particularly popular among the younger generation. This fact, in turn, has given rise to some nationalistic grumblings about supposed Yankee cultural imperialism. In some parts of the interior, musical forms of Indian origin still enjoy a certain popularity.

Architecture and the Plastic Arts

Argentina has not noticeably participated in the outburst of modern architecture so visible in such Latin American countries as Mexico and Brazil. Although Buenos Aires and other cities possess a number of private houses characteristic of modern trends in architecture, most private homes are built along conservative lines, adhering to the late nineteenth- and early twentieth-century models made popular by the immigrants from Spain and Italy. There is not a sufficient number of modern homes to speak of a change in the characteristic look of Buenos Aires and of other cities. The government has never particularly patronized modern architecture. During the early 1900's, the classical modes were most popular and served as style for such edifices as the Congress Building and the law courts in Buenos Aires. During the Perón regime, the government erected some buildings that were reminiscent and characteristic of the dictatorial architecture of the Hitler, Mussolini, and Stalin regimes in Europe.

The failure of Argentina to participate in the Latin American development of modern architecture was perhaps due to the fact that modern architecture began to be popular in Latin America when Argentina was undergoing its period of political instability. The Perón revolution favored heavy imperial-style architecture rather than architectural experimentation and innovation.

In the plastic arts, too, Argentina has not stood out among the Latin American nations. It has produced no Diego Riveras or Portinaris, has had no great sculptors and has therefore never developed anything comparable to the mural paintings on public buildings so characteristic of Mexico or to the Bienal of São Paulo where painters, sculptors, and architects exhibit their works.

Sports

Sports are an important part of any popular culture, and the Argentines tend to be avid sports fans. The newspapers carry a good deal of sports news, and the most recent sports contests are subject of avid conversations in restaurants and sidewalk cafes. The most popular sport is *futebol,* or soccer. Boys learn to play the game at an early age. The pictures of *futebol* stars take up considerable space in daily newspapers and popular magazines, and Argentine youngsters are as acquainted with the names of *futebol* stars as their counterparts in the United States are with current baseball heroes.

On the adult level, *futebol* is a highly organized sport, with professional teams, each of which has its avid supporters. Members of *futebol* teams are very well paid. Each Sunday afternoon, hundreds of thousands of spectators go to the large stadiums in Buenos Aires to see their favorite teams play and express their partisanship. In most other major cities and towns, the size of the stadiums corresponds more to the population of the place but with an equally frequent program of *futebol* games.

Another favorite sport is horse racing, which draws very large crowds on Sundays and special race days. The Argentines are very proud of the quality of their race horses, and a number of them have given a good account of themselves in racing in foreign countries, including the United States. A good deal of money is bet on the races in Argentina, but the same is true of the large *futebol* games.

Boxing, both amateur and professional, has its practitioners in Argentina; some have won international fame, including Firpo, "the wild bull of the pampas," who fought Jack Dempsey for the world heavyweight championship in the early 1920's. Basketball and tennis are less popular; baseball is nonexistent in Argentina.

Among upper-class Argentines, some other sports enjoy high prestige. These are principally of British origin, and the most important is polo. Argentina has produced very good polo players and teams that have done well in international competitions. Other British-introduced sports are golf and cricket, which have some practitioners and fans but are not widely popular even among the aristocracy.

Summary and Conclusions

During the first few decades of the twentieth century, Argentina enjoyed an unchallenged position as the cultural leader among the Latin American countries. Its high rate of literacy; its universities, which attracted students from all over the region; its publishing industry; its newspapers; and its literary figures were all responsible for this position of eminence. During recent decades, however, the political, economic, and social crisis of Argentina has had its negative impact also on the country's cultural activities. Although many Argentines remain ignorant of the fact that their country is no longer in the van of literary and artistic progress in the hemisphere, this is in fact the case.

Argentine publishing is now rivaled on a major scale by Mexican houses and to a lesser degree by firms in half a dozen other Latin American countries; most of the country's publishers have suffered from frequent harrassment by the dictatorial regimes since the 1930's. Argentine social scientists are fast being outpaced by those in Mexico and Brazil; and Argentine literature no longer has the pre-eminence it once enjoyed.

However, Argentina still possesses many cultural advantages. Its literacy level is high, its number of university graduates is large, and, on the whole, its publishing industry is still prosperous. A reasonable degree of political stability and a reburst of economic prosperity might help to re-establish Argentina's position as a cultural leader in Latin America.

VII

Argentina and the World

Two factors were traditionally fundamental in Argentina's relations with the rest of the world: its special relationship with Europe and its aspirations to be the leader of the Latin American nations. In recent decades, both these long-time elements of Argentina's international relations have changed. Its contacts with Europe have become much less important than they once were, while other Latin American nations have surpassed Argentina in influence and importance.

Argentine Orientation Toward Europe

For nearly three quarters of a century, Argentina's relations with Europe were particularly close. This was the result of at least three factors: its economic association with Great Britain; its cultural orientation toward France and, to a lesser degree, toward Spain and Germany; and its large-scale immigration, predominantly from southern Europe and especially from Italy and Spain.

With the opening of British markets to foodstuffs from abroad in the middle of the nineteenth century, Argentina's economy became closely integrated with that of Great Britain. Argentina became one of the principal suppliers of meat and grain to the British market and, in return, a consumer of a vast range of British manufactured goods. Argentine railroads were built almost as replicas of British railroads; the Bank of London and South America and various other British credit institutions played a major role in financing trade between the two countries; and even British-owned department stores, such as Gath and Chaves, sold imported British goods directly to the Argentine public. Thus, Argentine economic interests became closely entwined with those of Great Britain. The cattle and wheat growers of the pampas, who came to constitute the country's aristocracy and who, for long, dominated the government, were strongly pro-British out of self-interest. Argentina looked largely to Great Britain for innovations and advances in the economic field.

The British had also considerable cultural influence in Argentina. They introduced the Argentine aristocracy to polo and the masses to soccer, and large numbers of English words, sometimes in Hispanicized form, found their way into Argentine Spanish. Not infrequently, Buenos Aires publishers brought out translations of English books.

On the whole, however, the cultural impact of continental Europe was undoubtedly more pronounced than that of Great Britain. Particularly in the late nineteenth century, the influence of French literature was strong in Argentina, as was that of the contemporary French schools of painting and to some degree of French music. In the fields of social science and philosophy, German influence was of great importance, and German military missions were very influential in molding Argentine military thought.

After the final liquidation of the Spanish Empire at the end of the nineteenth century, Argentine intellectuals were strongly influenced by Spanish thought. And this element in the cultural life of Argentina undoubtedly contributed strongly to anti-British and anti-United States currents among Argentine intellectuals during the early decades of the twentieth century. It also led to some revision of the traditionally anti-Spanish bias that had characterized most Argentines since the struggles for independence a century earlier.

Immigration was another factor that tied Argentina closely to the Old World. Starting in the second half of the nineteenth century, millions of people migrated to Argentina from Europe. Although there were sizable numbers of immigrants from Germany and the Slavic countries, and even some from Great Britain and France, the overwhelming majority came from Italy and Spain. As a result of their influence, Buenos Aires and other coastal areas soon showed more of the atmosphere and appearance of European cities than of typical Latin American ones. As it happened, these immigrants played a very important cultural role; they also exercized considerable political influence. Italian and German language newspapers and reviews flourished, foreign-language benevolent societies were important social centers, and Italian literature had a wide audience in Argentina. Although only a native-born Argentine could aspire to the presidency of the republic, there were numerous senators, deputies, and lesser political dignities of foreign birth in Argentina during the first three decades of the twentieth century.

The Argentine crisis of the past years has arisen in part from the difficulty the country had in adjusting to the decline of European influence. Economically, Great Britain's influence has been partly supplanted by that of the United States. Culturally, Argentine intellectuals have increasingly turned inward to Argentine traditions and history rather than to Europe for their models and inspirations. At the same time, the immigrant stream has virtually dried up: the sons and daughters of the immigrants, the second generation Argentines, have tended to reject their parents' traditions as foreign, and Buenos Aires and other urban centers have suffered the impact of the migration from the interior of millions of rural workers and small townspeople, to whom the European orientation of the coast was alien.

Argentina's Traditional Role in America

Argentina's long-time orientation toward Europe was not unconnected with her traditional role in the Western Hemisphere. Ever since the latter decades of the nineteenth century, Argentina stood forth as the principal center of resistance to North American influence and power among the Latin American nations.

Argentina also looked upon the Inter-American System, which began with the First Pan-American Conference in 1890 and, in successive stages, produced the Bureau of American States, the Pan American Union, and finally, in 1948, the Organization of American States, with considerable skepticism.

Argentines took a leading part in developing the thesis of nonintervention. As early as 1868, Dr. Carlos Calvo, a leading Argentine jurist, published a treatise in which he argued strongly against the right of any American country to intervene in the internal affairs of another. In 1902, Argentine Foreign Minister Luis M. Drago denounced the use of force or the threat of force to attempt to collect private debts owed by a Latin American country or citizens of such a country. These principles were finally incorporated in the Good Neighbor Policy of the 1930's and thereafter.

Argentine opposition to the United States became obvious during World War I. In spite of the Argentine landowners' sympathies for Great Britain, the Conservative government, which was in power during the first two years of the war, maintained Argentine neutrality. In 1916, Hipólito Irigoyen, whose anti-British attitude was matched by his opposition to the United States, was elected president. He, too, insisted on maintaining Argentine neutrality, even though the United States and several Latin American countries became combatants on the side of the Allies after 1916.

During World War II, Argentina's opposition to U.S. leadership in hemispheric affairs became particularly marked. The government of President Ramón S. Castillo also maintained a position of neutrality during the early stages of the war; this neutrality, however, was more than benevolent toward the Axis Powers. The upshot of this policy was that Argentina resisted tenaciously all attempts by the United States to align the Latin American countries with the Allies in World War II. Argentina refused to break relations with the Axis, as almost all other Latin American countries did, even after Pearl Harbor, and it strongly resisted any suggestion that it actually join the Allied side in the conflict.

With the overthrow of President Castillo by pro-German military men in June, 1943, the position of Argentina became even more pro-Axis. There is evidence that the Argentine military actually gave considerable help to German submarines operating in South Atlantic waters during this period. It was only under the most extreme pressure of the United States that the government of General Pedro Ramírez finally broke off formal diplomatic relations with the Axis Powers in February, 1944, but even this act did not end cooperation between the Argentine military and their German counterparts. Finally, and only under the threat that Argentina would not be admitted to the United Nations and that it might be excluded from the Inter-American Conference at Chapultepec, Mexico, did Argentina declare war on the Axis early in 1945, when it was clear that the Germans had been defeated.

Argentina wanted to be much more than merely negative in inter-American relations; it aspired to leadership among the Latin American nations, and this not only in opposition to the United States but in other ways as well.

Successive Argentine governments participated actively in the so-called ABC block, consisting of Argentina, Brazil, and Chile. On many occasions, this group served as an intermediary between the United States and the nations in and around the Caribbean. In several instances, it even played a role in the domestic conflicts in these countries, notably during the sanguinary early years (1910–20) of the Mexican Revolution.

The Aspirations of the Perón Regime

During the early years of the Perón regime, the aspiration of the Perón government for Argentina's role in hemispheric and world affairs soared. Before his overthrow in September, 1955, all these aspirations had been thwarted, and the true decline of Argentine influence in American and in world affairs had begun to become evident. Perón did not only desire a leading role in the Western Hemisphere but also in the world at large. To attain this position, he sought to employ two factors: the favorable economic position then enjoyed by Argentina and the "philosophy" of his regime.

Argentina emerged from World War II with a very advantageous position for making its weight felt in hemispheric and world affairs. It had been untouched by the war, and as the result of large demands for the country's basic export products during the conflict, it had very large foreign-exchange balances available in both Great Britain and the United States. In addition, for some years after the war, the demand for Argentina exports was exceedingly high, and, nominally at least, Argentina could get very high prices for its products. And finally, in the late 1940's, Argentina had a better developed industry than almost all other Latin American countries.

Perón sought to use these temporary advantages to the utmost. First, he employed some resources to further strengthen and diversify the Argentine economy. Second, Perón tried to gain influence in Europe through negotiations over the placing of Argentine exports, and as a result, Spain was largely dependent on Argentine meat and grain for its food supply at a time when the Allies were subjecting the Franco regime to an economic boycott. France, Italy, and other Western European countries were also dependent to some degree on Argentine exports, while the normal reliance of Britain on Argentina for meat and wheat was intensified.

A third method by which Perón sought to use his advantageous economic position in the late 1940's was through enticing Argentina's neighbors into close association with and dependence on Argentina. He made grandiose offers to put Argentina's allegedly unlimited resources at the disposal of the rest of Latin America if the United States refused to provide aid for the economic development of these nations.

Negotiations were undertaken with Chile, Paraguay, and Bolivia with a view toward establishing customs unions with these countries. The agreements that were negotiated not only provided for large increases in trade but also for heavy Argentine public and private investments in these countries.

A high point in Perón's attempt to use economic affluence to obtain hemispheric political leadership was the Bogotá Conference in 1948, at which the Organization of American States (OAS) was established. The Latin American delegates to that conference pressed hard with the U.S. representatives for the establishment of the Inter-American Bank to help finance the economic-development efforts of the various Latin American countries. When the U.S. delegation made it very clear that it had no intention of supporting such an institution, the Argentines announced that if the United States would not finance the bank, Argentina would be willing and able to do so.

The Perón regime supplemented its economic influence with an attempt to spread Argentine political influence in the hemisphere and in the world at large. For this purpose, some Peronista intellectuals formulated the *justicialista* philosophy. Although a somewhat jerry-built ideology, *justicialismo* was essentially a third-force philosophy. Perón and his advisers argued that the underdeveloped countries of the world really had little interest in the rapidly developing Cold War between the United States and the Soviet Union, that neither Communism nor capitalism was an adequate social and economic system for them, and that they should seek some intermediary arrangement that would combine the best elements of both systems.

With this end in view, Perón dispatched, in 1947, a series of public letters to important world figures, including Pope Pius XII and Jawaharlal Nehru, then recently installed Prime Minister of India, urging them to join him in organizing a third force in the world. At the same time, he undertook a vigorous campaign throughout Latin America to popularize *justicialismo* and to assert Argentine leadership.

One of his first moves was to dispatch labor attachés to all Argentine embassies in the Western Hemisphere. Their function was to propagandize the virtues of the Perón system and to recruit loyal foreign followers, particularly among the organized-labor movement. At the same time, the Eva Perón Welfare Foundation, which had been given a monopoly of charitable activities in Argentina, was used to make gifts at strategic times and places in Latin America. The gifts were administered by the labor attachés.

Somewhat later, Perón sought to build an Argentine-led continental labor confederation. This group, the Agrupación de Trabajadores Latino Americanos Sindicalizados (ATLAS), was established in 1952 and became a very vociferous and for a time exceedingly well financed arm of Argentine foreign policy in the hemisphere. ATLAS and the CGT also entered into contact with some labor groups in other parts of the world, including the Egyptian unions and the so-called unions of Franco's Spain, looking toward the possibility of organizing a world labor confederation which, hopefully, would be under Peronista leadership.

Perón supplemented his labor efforts with attempts to influence the political parties and the military in various Latin American countries. His party efforts were particularly intense in Chile, where, Perón supported, perhaps with considerable financial help, General Carlos Ibañez in his campaign for the Chilean presidency in 1952. Perón was especially active in financing the Partido Feminista Chileno, a women's party, which was one of Ibañez' principal backers. However, during a visit to Chile one year after Ibañez' election, Perón succeeded in alienating virtually all his supporters in that country and almost completely destroyed his previously substantial influence. Perón also established fairly close relations with João Goulart, Brazil's minister of labor in 1953–54 and political heir to ex-dictator Getulio Vargas. During the early 1950's, Peronista political influence was also significant in Colombia and Venezuela.

The Argentine military was also used by Perón. There was some indication of Peronista cooperation with military coups in Peru and Venezuela in 1948, and thereafter the Argentine regime collaborated more or less closely with the military dictators General Manuel Odría and General Marcos Pérez Jiménez. Perón took refuge in Venezuela for a while after he was overthrown in 1955. Peronistas also gave considerable advice to General Gustavo Rojas Pinilla, dictator of Colombia from 1953 to 1957.

Perón's Failure

By the time Perón was overthrown, the international house of cards, which he had constructed during his early years in power, had collapsed. His efforts to gain influence in Europe through the judicious placing of Argentine exports had come to naught, since, with the disappearance of Argentina's large export surpluses after 1949, the Perón regime found that it had no influence at all in Spain, Italy, or France. Those countries had been willing to treat Perón as an equal so long as they needed him, but thereafter they made it clear that they did not really regard him as such.

Much the same happened with Perón's economic campaign in Latin America. Although Paraguay and Bolivia ratified the customs-union treaties they had signed with Perón's representatives, these agreements were never actually put into effect. The Chilean Congress, however, refused to ratify the two agreements that successive Chilean governments had negotiated with Perón. The Argentine promise at the Bogotá Conference to finance an Inter-American Bank turned out to be an empty boast, since, within a year of that date, Argentina had exhausted its foreign-exchange reserves and was facing a mounting balance-of-payments crisis.

The political endeavors of the Perón regime did not fare much better, since the efforts of the labor attachés produced relatively sparse results. In the few countries in which Argentina's envoys were able to gain some influence in the labor movements, it ultimately proved to be ephemeral. ATLAS turned out to be a weak reed, being able to obtain the affiliation of no major national labor group outside of Argentina. When, in 1953, Perón and Milton Eisenhower reached an agreement on U.S. aid to Argentina, the Perón regime stopped its violent anti-American campaign, thus depriving ATLAS of one of its main stocks in trade.

Peronista liaison with political groups in various Latin American countries did not prosper any more than did the regime's activities in the trade-union area. Even before the overthrow of Perón, almost all Peronista influence in Chile had been destroyed largely as a result of the Argentine president's visit to that country in 1953. After Perón's overthrow, little contact was maintained with political groups in Peru, Colombia, and other countries where there had been some *justicialista* following in the early 1950's.

Also the work done by the Argentine military on behalf of Perón did not survive the overthrow of his regime. In fact, the Latin American military dictators who had worked closely with Perón—Odría in Peru, Pérez Jiménez in Venezuela, and Trujillo in the Dominican Republic—were all overthrown within six years of Perón's own downfall.

On balance, Perón's efforts to obtain wide international influence bore little fruit; they may have even weakened Argentina's general international position. Among some of Argentina's neighbors they aroused fear of a new imperialism emanating from Buenos Aires. Perón's unfilled boasts and promises made his regime, and perhaps his country, appear slightly ridiculous.

Argentina and the United States

For some decades, the official attitude of Argentine governments and of many politicians toward the United States has been somewhat schizophrenic. Since U.S. economic influence in Argentina tended to be small and much surpassed by that of Great Britain, most of the resentment against economic imperialism was centered on Great Britain rather than on the United States. This was particularly reflected in the 1930's when the governments of that period made agreements with the British which tended to hamper the industrialization of Argentina. It was also reflected in the establishment of IAPI by the Perón government, supposedly to prevent British buyers from taking advantage of Argentina in sales of Argentine exports in the post-World War II period.

However, it was the United States that blocked the persistent aspiration of the successive Argentine regimes to become the leader of the Latin American nations. In recent years, the economic, political, and cultural influence of the United States in the hemisphere, and in Argentina, has grown, while that of Great Britain has declined. As a result, there has been increasing resentment against U.S. economic power as well as against U.S. opposition to Argentine aspirations to hegemony in the hemisphere.

During the Perón period, Argentine hostility toward the United States was particularly intense. In his first election campaign, Perón used the slogan "Braden or Perón," to picture the campaign as a struggle between the recent U.S. ambassador who had been outspoken in his opposition to Perón and Perón himself, as one of his most potent election slogans. During his first eight years in office, Perón maintained his violent anti-U.S. attitude. However, during his last three years, this position was much muted.

Perón's successors were more friendly toward the United States. Presidents Lonardi and Aramburu looked to the U.S. for financial aid to reconstruct the Argentine economy, and their administrations made no pretense to asserting their nation's leadership in Latin America.

The attitude of President Arturo Frondizi toward the United States was somewhat more complicated. He was anxious to free Argentina from the remains of its traditional economic dependence on Great Britain and tried to do so through a program of industrialization. For this, however, he needed extensive help both from U.S. private investors and from the U.S. government. Frondizi also felt a political kinship with President John F. Kennedy, who came to power about half-way through Frondizi's tenure in office, as well as with other left-democratic regimes in Latin America that were kindly disposed toward the Kennedy administration. President Kennedy reciprocated Frondizi's attitude and sought Argentina's cooperation.

None of the post-Frondizi governments was willing or able to adopt the hostile attitude which had characterized the Perón regime. All were dependent on the United States for help in dealing with Argentina's continuing economic crisis. At the same time, the weakness of the economy deprived them of a sufficient basis for standing up decisively against any U.S. policies or attitudes with which they might have disagreed.

Argentina's Relations with Its Neighbors

Argentina's political and economic influence has, understandably, been greatest in the nations that border it, although these countries—Paraguay, Uruguay, Bolivia, and Chile—have generally been of two minds about their more powerful neighbor. They have admired the cosmopolitan atmosphere of Buenos Aires and the relatively high standard of living that most Argentines enjoy, but they have also been fearful of becoming victims of "Argentine imperialism."

Paraguay is the country that has traditionally been most under Argentine influence. Argentine investors have developed Paraguay's yerba mate industry, have provided most of its banking services, and have handled most of its foreign commerce. To a large degree, Paraguay has been at the mercy of Argentina because the rivers that provide most of its contact with the outside world pass through Argentina. It is virtually an axiom of Paraguayan politics that a government that does not have at least the passive acceptance of the rulers in Buenos Aires cannot remain in power very long.

Since Uruguay has direct access to the sea, it has been considerably less dependent upon Argentina than its up-river neighbor, although Argentine investment in Uruguay has been extensive and Argentine wheat has traditionally supplied most of Uruguay's needs. In recent decades, Argentine tourists have also played an important part in the Uruguayan economy.

The contrast between Uruguayan democracy and Argentine political instability and frequent dictatorial rule has been a prime source of friction between the two countries since 1930. Exiles from Argentine dictatorships most often find refuge in Montevideo. During the Perón regime, the Argentine Government showed its resentment of Uruguay's willingness to harbor exiles by forbidding all Argentines to vacation at the Uruguayan beaches and by banning export of Argentine wheat to Uruguay.

Bolivia has also felt Argentine's influence, and Bolivians fear possible Argentine territorial ambitions directed toward the southern sections of their republic. Argentina has frequently interfered in the internal political affairs of Bolivia, often financing expeditions of Bolivian exiles who wish to overthrow the current Bolivian regime, and has also used economic pressure in trying to force Bolivian governments to do its bidding. As a result, although the Bolivians were anxious to have the Argentines build a railroad connecting Buenos Aires with La Paz, successive Bolivian regimes have exercised great caution in granting their neighbors the right to exploit oil and mineral resources near Bolivia's southern border.

The relationship of Argentina and Chile has been somewhat different. Since Chile is stronger both economically and politically than most of Argentina's other neighbors, Argentine economic penetration has been minor. However, for more than half a century, a deep-seated suspicion of Argentina has existed on the other side of the Andes. Continuing border disputes and occasional clashes between the armed forces of the two countries have helped to disrupt their relations.

During the Perón regime, Chilean fears of Argentina were particularly marked. However, for a short time in the early 1950's, Perón succeeded in winning considerable sympathy among the workers of Chile, on the basis of the social legislation he had enacted in Argentina. This feeling soon disappeared when Perón made a state visit to Chile and behaved as if Chile were one more Argentine province. Since the overthrow of Perón, relations between the two countries have generally been correct, if not particularly cordial.

A special word needs to be said concerning Argentine-Brazilian relations. As the two largest and most powerful nations of South America, these countries have naturally been jealous of one another. During the first half of the nineteenth century, they fought each other on various occasions until Uruguay was established as an independent country to serve as a buffer between them.

Different attitudes toward the United States and its influence in the hemisphere also kept Argentina and Brazil apart

for many decades. While Brazil considered itself a U.S. ally
and an intermediary between the United States and the Latin
American countries, Argentina was traditionally chief spokesman of the opposition to U.S. ambitions. As a rule, Argentines have always felt superior to the Brazilians and have
looked down on their northern neighbors as being "tropical,"
poor, and lazy. However, in the last several decades, most
Argentines have become much less sure of their superiority.
While Brazil's economy was expanding with great rapidity,
that of Argentina was virtually stagnant; while Brazil surged
ahead in cultural achievement, Argentina's leadership in this
field was eroding; and, while Brazil increasingly played a
leadership role in inter-American affairs, Argentina's position of pre-eminence was disappearing.

The Decline of Argentina's International Position

Argentina's international prestige and influence is less in
the late 1960's than it was a generation ago, since its economic importance, cultural impact, and political prestige
have fared badly during the intervening period. Whereas
Argentina's economy has largely stagnated during the last
few decades, those of most other Latin American countries
have developed rapidly. Mexico and Brazil, for example, have
far surpassed Argentina in terms of economic development.
Also the economic distance between Argentina and many
of the smaller Latin American countries, such as Venezuela,
Colombia, or Peru, has greatly narrowed. Today, Argentina
is only one of seven Latin American countries possessing an
integrated steel industry, and those of Mexico and Brazil
have a productive capacity considerably greater than that of
Argentina. Furthermore, Argentina is only one of four countries containing an extensive petrochemical industry, and
those of Mexico, Brazil, and Venezuela are expanding much
more rapidly than that of Argentina. Similarly, agricultural

production is rising rapidly in Mexico and Venezuela, while it is stagnant in Argentina.

The cultural importance of Argentina in Latin America is also considerably less than thirty years ago. The publishing firms of Mexico have a wider distribution of books than those of Argentina, and many of the smaller Latin American countries have also developed extensive publishing industries. Argentina has shared little in the architectural renaissance that has taken place in Latin America since World War II. The fame of Argentine universities has been seriously impaired by successive purges during and since the Perón period, while universities in several other Latin American countries have expanded dramatically.

Finally, Argentina can no longer be regarded as the spokesman for the Latin American countries in international politics and diplomacy. Since the late 1930's, Mexico has paved the way for Latin America to follow a foreign policy independent of the United States. Mexico has consistently opposed any intervention by an American nation in the domestic affairs of any other American country. It has followed a course of its own choosing both in the United Nations and in the OAS and has done so without perturbing its friendly relations with the United States. Argentina, however, has lost all consistency in its dealings with the great neighbor of the north. Argentina's chronic political instability has greatly lowered the country's prestige in Latin America. Even those Latin American nations that have suffered from the same ills as Argentina have not been able to turn to Argentina for guidance or encouragement in their efforts to achieve a more orderly political behavior, and those that have gained a certain degree of political stability have increasingly tended to look upon the situation in Argentina as a horrid example of what they would like to avoid.

Conclusion

As we have seen in the foregoing pages, Argentina's problem is one of thwarted change and development. The lingering crisis from which the nation has suffered is fundamentally political and involves two basic issues: first, how to provide leadership for completing the process of social change and economic development that has been halted in midstream, and second, how to bridge the gulf which divides the Argentine people into Peronistas and anti-Peronistas.

There is little question that, once the political deadlock has been broken, Argentina has the potentialities to assume a major leadership position in Latin America. The richness of its soil, the prevalence of oil, and at least a modest endowment of minerals provide the base for the development of a prosperous and diversified modern agricultural-industrial economy. The size of the population and the fact that most of the people are incorporated in the money economy provides a relatively sizable market, which will undoubtedly be supplemented if Argentina is able in the future to sell more advanced industrial products to some of the other Latin American nations.

Furthermore, Argentina's population is one of the country's most important resources. Living in a generally healthy climate and lacking the racial divisions that plague other Latin American nations, the generally literate Argentines have a reservoir of skills and a basic educational system capable of generating new skills that are matched by few, if any, other countries of the area.

It seems unlikely that Argentina will, in the foreseeable future, be ranked among the world's great powers, as seems to be the destiny of its neighbor Brazil, which has a much larger territory, more ample resources, and a very much greater population. However, Argentina, along with Canada, Mexico, and several other countries, certainly has the capacity to join the group of intermediate powers that is likely to play a growing role in global affairs.

In the meanwhile, and at least temporarily, Argentina is caught in a dead-end. The cycle of coups and countercoups goes on; the infrastructure of the economy continues to deteriorate; and the nation's cultural and scientific possibilities are reduced by the insecurity derived from political instability, insufficient financial resources resulting from the nearly stagnated economy, and a serious flow of talents abroad.

Most Argentines have been puzzled, hurt, and frustrated by their country's apparent inability to resolve its lingering crisis. For a few, the frustration has been so great as to convince them that no solution is possible until their nation has been "cleansed" by a guerrilla and civil war destroying all existing social and political institutions. Fortunately, the Argentines driven to this degree of desperation are still very few in number and, as yet, quite ineffective.

The overwhelming majority of Argentines remains moderately hopeful that a peaceful and democratic solution can be found to their nation's dilemma. However, one thing appears certain: A democratic resolution of the situation seems unlikely so long as Juan Domingo Perón is still alive. Even the remotest possibility that the ex-dictator might return to power is likely to frustrate the most sincere attempt to incorporate the Peronistas into the country's political life. But such a possibility will continue to exist—at least in the minds of the anti-Peronistas—so long as Perón lives.

Once the possibility of Perón's return has been definitely

eliminated, Argentina will probably find a way out of this apparently unbreakable vicious circle, although one would be rash to predict a particular party or leader that could do so. Yet there are many factors that indicate that the deadlock can be broken. First, a considerable degree of industrialization has occurred, albeit slowly, since the end of the last rural-aristocratic regime in 1943. The idea that the process of industrialization must go on is now accepted by the great majority of politically conscious Argentines, and future political leaders who hope to gain the support of that majority will undoubtedly strongly support industrialization. Second, the Peronista revolution did make the urban and rural working classes a major force in national politics. Even more importantly, it gave the workers a feeling of their own dignity and importance, and future political leaders will find it necessary to allow wide participation of the workers in the political process. Furthermore, even the most obdurate anti-Peronista politicians have come to realize that, for a long time to come, some version of the Peronista Party will continue to represent the majority of the workers, both organized and unorganized.

For their part, few Peronistas, whether of the leadership or of the rank and file, want to establish a dictatorship. Increasingly, they have come to admit the evils of dictatorial rule and to seek the firm establishment of a democratic regime, which their party will hopefully participate in as leader.

Finally, the military leaders have become increasingly aware of the dangers to the armed forces resulting from the latter's constant incursion into politics. Many soldiers have favored a return to the barracks, but the ever-present dread of Perón's possible return has nonetheless, on several occasions since 1955, convinced even generals who favored a return to more strictly professional activities that they must intervene "just once more." Perón's disappearance should ultimately remove this dread of coup and countercoup.

Other factors may develop before the demise of Perón

which could change this cautiously optimistic outlook expressed here. However, barring such an eventuality, there is substantial reason to believe that Argentina will experience during the last quarter of the twentieth century much more rapid economic progress, much greater material well-being for its populace, and much greater internal stability and democratic political life than has marked its history during the middle years of this century. Argentina may well become once again a country admired and studied as an example of how to resolve grave economic, social, and political problems rather than as a case study of errors and evils to be avoided.

Bibliographic Note

Much of the material contained in these pages is drawn from the author's observation of Argentine affairs over more than two decades. However, a good deal was also gleaned from other sources on Argentina. Hence, this bibliographic note is designed to indicate sources used as well as to give suggestions for further reading on Argentina.

In recent years, several foreign authors have presented short over-all views of Argentina. Each of these volumes is valuable, each takes a somewhat different point of view, and each concentrates on particular aspects of the Argentine scene. Thus, Arthur Whitaker's *Argentina* (Englewood Cliffs, N.J.: Prentice-Hall, 1964) is particularly concerned with the emergence of nationalism. James Scobie's *Argentina: A City and a Nation* (New York: Oxford University Press, 1964) looks at the country in terms of the eternal conflict between Buenos Aires and the rest of the nation. George Pendle's *Argentina* (London: Royal Institute of International Affairs, 1963) is, in turn, particularly concerned with the economic and political development of the country.

Another fairly general approach to the problems of Argentina is provided by James Bruce's *Those Perplexing Argentines* (New York: Longmans, Green & Co., 1953). Mr. Bruce was U.S. ambassador to Argentina during the Perón period, and tends to focus on the events of that period and particularly upon his own experiences in Argentina.

Undoubtedly, the Perón era has drawn most attention from recent writers, both national and foreign. Perhaps the two best books on this period are George Blansten's *Perón's Argentina*

(Chicago: University of Chicago Press, 1953) and Robert J. Alexander's *The Perón Era* (New York: Columbia University Press, 1951). The former emphasizes Perón's attempt to evolve a particular social and political philosophy for his regime, while the latter concentrates on the important role played by labor during the Peronista period.

Several other books on the Peronista period are also of interest. These include Arthur Whitaker's *The United States and Argentina* (Cambridge, Mass.: Harvard University Press, 1959), which centers on the relations of the Perón regime with the United States; María Flores' excellent study of Evita Perón called *Woman with the Whip* (New York: Doubleday & Co., 1952); and *Nuestros Vecinos Justicialistas* (Santiago, Chile: Editorial Pacifico, 1955), a critical study by the Chilean politician and social scientist Alejandro Magnet.

Other aspects of the Argentine scene have been dealt with by a variety of authors. The best readily available sources of information about the country's geography is Preston James's *Latin America* (New York: Odyssey Press, 1959). The Argentine historian and politician José Luis Romero has written two important books on the evolution of Argentina's political ideas. The first was originally published in Mexico in 1946 and has been translated into English by Thomas McGann as *A History of Argentine Political Thought* (Stanford, Calif.: Stanford University Press, 1963). The second book is *El Desarrollo de las Ideas en la Sociedad Argentina del Siglo XX,* published in Mexico (Fondo de Cultura Económica), in 1965.

Two further books on Argentine history might be of interest to the reader. One is Ricardo Levene's *A History of Argentina* (Chapel Hill, N.C.: University of North Carolina Press, 1937), which concentrates on the colonial period and on the struggle for independence; the second is Ysabel Rennie's *The Argentine Republic* (New York: The Macmillan Co., 1945), which deals especially with the economic growth of the country in the latter part of the nineteenth and the early part of the twentieth century. An important example of a somewhat biased discussion of the early forces that shaped the Argentine national character is Domingo Sarmiento's famous *Facundo,* which has been published in many Spanish but no recent English editions.

So far, surprisingly little has been written which seriously attempts to investigate the causes of Argentina's recent economic and political stagnation. An interesting, although not entirely satisfying attempt at such an explanation is offered by Tomás Robert Filiol's *Social Factors in Economic Development: The Argentine Case* (Cambridge, Mass.: MIT Press, 1961). Another explanation is given by William Withers in his *The Economic Crisis in Latin America* (New York: The Free Press, 1964). Withers argues that the root of the problem lies in the Argentine attempt to industrialize, a point of view with which this author does not agree.

An interesting and instructive book on early Argentine foreign policy is Thomas F. McGann's *Argentina, the United States and the Inter American System* (Cambridge, Mass.: Harvard University Press, 1957). *The Organization of American States* (Dallas, Texas: Southern Methodist University Press, 1963) by Ann Van Wynn Thomas and A. J. Thomas, Jr., also contains much material on Argentine attitudes toward the United States and the Inter-American system.

If one wishes to keep abreast of current developments in Argentina, one can get some help from newspapers such as *The New York Times, The Christian Science Monitor,* and *The Washington Post.* However, the reader would want to supplement these sources with information contained from time to time in such journals of opinion as *The Nation, The New Republic, The New Leader,* and *The National Review.* In addition, he might want to consult the Arizona State University's *Latin American Digest,* which attempts to provide, in capsule form, a running account of events in Argentina and in all other Latin American countries. For more analytical material, the *Hispanic American Historical Review, The Journal of Latin American Studies,* and *Inter American Economic Affairs* are valuable sources.

Index

189